Criminal Justice
Recent Scholarship

Edited by
Nicholas P. Lovrich

A Series from LFB Scholarly

Penal Sanctioning in the United States
Explaining Cross-State Differences

Frederique A. Laubepin

LFB Scholarly Publishing LLC
El Paso 2015

Library of Congress Cataloging-in-Publication Data

Library of Congress Cataloging-in-Publication Data

Laubepin, Frederique A., 1975-
  Penal sanctioning in the United States : explaining cross-state
differences / Frederique A. Laubepin.
      pages cm. -- (Criminal justice: recent scholarship)
  Includes bibliographical references and index.
  ISBN 978-1-59332-768-2 (hardcover : alk. paper)
  1. Imprisonment--United States--States. 2. Prison sentences--United
States--States. 3. Corrections--United States--States. 4. Criminal
justice, Administration of--United States--States. 5. Discrimination in
criminal justice administration--United States--States. I. Title.
  HV9471.L38 2015
  365'.973--dc23
                                        2014038908

ISBN 978-1-59332-768-2

A mes parents, Jean et Jacqueline,
et à ma soeur Mathilde,
pour l'amour, la foi, la patience, et le dévouement
dont ils ont fait preuve.

Table of Contents

List of Figures

List of Tables

Acknowledgements

I was able to complete this study only because I was able to stand on the broad and strong shoulders of others — those who have gone before me and paved the way. In addition to my family, who have always nurtured my dreams and supported my goals unconditionally, some exceptional people have lifted me so that I may reach higher than I could have on my own, guided and supported me through the difficulties of serious research, and believed in me when I did not believe in myself. They are giants all as far as I am concerned.

I am very grateful for the guidance provided by Jeffrey Morenoff, David Harding, David Thacher, and Anthony Chen. Although I could not hope to meet the high standards of their own research, it was a goal toward which I could work, and their remarkable achievements were a great source of inspiration. I am especially grateful to Jeffrey Morenoff for (ever so patiently and painstakingly) helping me to navigate the daunting world of statistics, build model after model, and think through their results. Working with him over the last few years has undoubtedly made me a better scholar.

I have been fortunate to come across other exceptional people who, each in their own way, have altered my life and career for the better and are deserving of recognition: Joe Fugate, who invited me to spend a year at Kalamazoo College where I met Kim Cummings and Robert Stauffer, whose passion for sociology was simply contagious; Bernard Bensoussan, of Université Lyon II, who opened the world of French sociology to me and challenged me to engage with it; and perhaps most of all my Khâgne English professor, Roger Buisine, who made me fall in love with the English language and appreciate the window that it offers into this culture. His exceptional instruction made it possible for me to pursue my dreams halfway across the world and yet, somehow, feel right at home.

I owe much to the students I taught at the University of Michigan, especially those who took my sociology of punishment classes and engaged with the material so enthusiastically. I may have learned more from them than they did from me. Being their instructor was the most challenging, inspiring, and rewarding experience of my early professional life.

In nearly every way, this book would not have been possible without the unwavering support and generosity of Dr. Lynette Hoelter, who not only gave me a job at the Inter-university Consortium for Political and Social Research, but has been my champion, mentor, role-model, and constant friend. I can never repay her kindness.

Chapter 1
Introduction

One of the defining characteristics of the late twentieth century social, political and cultural life in the United States has been an intense focus on the "crime problem" — urban violent crime, especially — and the unprecedented expansion of the penal system designed to contain it. Starting in the 1970s, prison populations grew sharply through the 1990s. By the end of 2007, U.S. prisons and jails held over 2.29 million men and women — a five-fold increase since 1972 and a rate six to ten times that of most comparable countries. All this growth took place in spite of declining crime rates. In 2007, the national incarceration rate reached 773 per 100,000 U.S. residents, up from 150 in 1972. New prison admissions contributed substantially to this increase, but so did parole revocations; in 1980 18 percent of prison populations were parolees returned to incarceration, but by 2000, this percentage had reached that of over a third (34 percent) (Travis 2007). This aspect of the mass incarceration phenomenon contributed to a dynamic variously referred to as the "revolving door" or the "catch and release (and catch again)" process. By all accounts, the breadth and size of this prison explosion have been nothing short of stunning, and a very substantial body of research has been devoted to exploring the causes, contours, and societal consequences of a phenomenon that has strained state and national correctional resources and has had a concentrated impact on minorities and the poor (Clear 2007; Jacobson 2006; Mauer and King 2007; Pager 2007; Western 2006).

A NEW PENOLOGICAL PARADIGM?

The prevailing and nearly uncontested narrative of the prison boom in the criminological literature tells the story of an extraordinarily punitive country in the throes of conservative vengeful ideology, building more and more prisons to incarcerate ever greater numbers of its citizens, most notably among the poor and non-White. This "punitive turn" (Garland 2001), a radical transformation in contemporary penality characterized by a perceived surge in punitiveness, is held responsible for the adoption of a long list of new, harsh, crime control policies in the United States and other Western countries:

> "harsher sentencing and increased use of imprisonment, 'three strikes' and mandatory minimum sentencing laws; 'truth-in-sentencing' and parole release restrictions; 'no frills' prison laws and 'austere prisons'; retribution in juvenile court and the imprisonment of children; the revival of chain gangs and corporal punishment; boot camps and supermax prisons; the multiplication of capital offenses and executions; community notification laws and pedophile registers; zero tolerance policies and Anti-Social Behavior Orders" (Garland 2001: 142).

It is tempting to see these changes as a radical break from the past, a new penological paradigm. To be sure, the far-reaching quantitative changes in the use of incarceration over the course of the last forty years have been accompanied by equally profound shifts in penal discourse, techniques, and objectives. After operating for a century under a positivist model, the criminal justice system saw its philosophical principles come under sharp attack as penal welfarism/modernism and the rehabilitative ideal came under scrutiny in the 1970s. Prior to the 1970s, the goal of rehabilitation was widely accepted as a legitimate objective of incarceration. However, the 1970s saw a dramatic shift in the power balance between the competing goals of rehabilitation and retributive punishment (Andrews and Bonta 1998; Cullen and Gendreau 1989). As crime increased rather dramatically, criminology experts, corrections practitioners, and the American public became equally disillusioned with the apparent lack of effectiveness of commonplace rehabilitation programs (Cullen, Fischer and Applegate 2000). The backlash against rehabilitation was further amplified by Martinson's (1974) influential review, which became synonymous with the 'nothing works' doctrine in criminal justice. As Garland (2001) explains,

> "[t]his fall from grace of rehabilitation was hugely significant. Its decline was the first indication that the modernist framework ... was coming undone. Rehabilitation had been the field's central structural support, the keystone in an arch of mutually supportive practices and ideologies. When faith in this ideal collapsed, it began to unravel the whole fabric of assumptions, values and practices upon which modern penality had been built." (8)

Accompanied by growing levels of insecurity and fear of crime, the focus turned from the rehabilitation of offenders to crime prevention (policing), risk management, and deterrence and retribution through the use of punitive sanctions.

Scholars have articulated a number of explanations for the punitive turn, focusing on processes that, individually or in combination, are seen as playing a key role the advent of the new penological paradigm: the decline of welfarism and the rehabilitative ideal, the 'disembedding' of social relations, the fragmenting of communities, and the emergence of new styles of managerialism, to name but a few (Matthews 2005). Thus for Loïc Wacquant (2000, 2004, 2005, 2009) the ascendancy of the penal state stems from the "generalization of insecurity" created by the neoliberal project (itself characterized by economic deregulation, increasing economic inequality, and the fragmentation of wage labor) as well as the upending of racial hierarchies in the post-civil rights era. The increasingly punitive management of the poor that takes place in reaction to this insecurity through the twin phenomena of social welfare reform on the one hand, and penal expansion and control on the other — or as Wacquant puts it, "the wedding of social and penal policy at the bottom of the polarized class structure" (2009: 304) — is seen as a "major *structural innovation*" (emphasis in original) designed to keep poor African Americans "in their place." David Garland (2001) also claims that we are witnessing a major transformation, but he attributes it instead to a crisis at the level of the state and to changes in the professional middle-classes. Once key supporters of penal welfarism, Garland argues, this social group has experienced "ontological insecurity" over the last several decades and, as a consequence, it has become a major influence in the populist current in penal politics. In a similar fashion, John Pratt (2002) contends that "the indifference of the general public is increasingly giving way to intolerance and demands for still greater manifestations of repressive punishment" (2002: 182). He sees this populist punitiveness from an Eliasean perspective as a "de-civilizing" influence on punishment, promoting disturbing, "more ostentatious and emotive" forms of punishment. Feeley and Simon (1992), like Wacquant, Garland, and others, note that the late modern era has been marked by a growing division between mainstream society and the "underclass" and they, too, see this as a key influence on penal policy. However, as they see it, the paradigm shift revolves not around punitiveness, but around managerialism. They delineate three characteristics of the postmodern penal era: (1) rather than the transformation of offenders into pro-social citizens, the new penal discourse emphasizes risk and probability as applied to offenders, with (2) the objective being to protect the public and manage criminals through (3) the implementation of efficient techniques (drug testing, electronic monitoring, …), actuarial methods (sentencing guidelines) to evaluate, classify, and control risk. The new penology, then, is "neither about punishing nor rehabilitating individuals … it is about identifying and managing unruly groups" (Feeley and Simon 1992: 455). This, they argue, is what distinguishes the "new penology" from the "old penology" of earlier periods.

In recent years however several commentators have challenged the prevailing consensus that the late modern penological developments constitute a radical break from the past. As Matthews (2005), Lynch (2011), Campbell and Schoenfeld (2013), and others point out, scholars of the punitive turn tend to over-emphasize differences between this and previous penological periods. Their accounts suffer from a "one-sided, exaggerated focus on punitiveness" (Matthews 2005: 175) that plays down "non-punitive" developments within penal policy and conveniently glosses over the fact that, historically, punishment has always had a symbolic, emotive, and expressive function, and the targets of formal social control have always been the poor and marginalized, the "lumpenproletariat," the "dangerous classes." "Can we fully distinguish past versions of penal cruelty and neglect of the poor from the contemporary versions?" Lynch asks. "Might even the albeit fractured and stingy US version of [penal] welfarism of the early to mid-20th century be the historical anomaly, and neglect and/or punitive intervention be the cultural norm to which we have returned?" (2011: 242). Rather than being indicative of the formation of a new, post-modern penal order then, it is more likely that the changes we are witnessing mark the continuation and acceleration (facilitated by advances in statistics and computer technology) of trends that may date back several hundred years.[1] As Lynch would put it, what we may have here is "an old power with some new tricks up its sleeve," an expanding and increasingly complex apparatus of crime control relying on a range of old and new interventionist strategies.

FIFTY-ONE DIFFERENT COUNTRIES?

Macro-level theories of the punitive turn also tend to produce monolithic analyses that over-simplify the history of the penological transformations that took place in the United States in the nineteenth and twentieth century. The dominant narrative of penal modernism portrays rehabilitation as the dominant and universally accepted ideology that shaped penal policy and practice "largely without dissent" (Zimring and Hawkins 1995: 7):

> "Rehabilitation was the law's stated objective in the criminal justice system and remained the dominant ideology in the architecture of the model penal code reforms of the 1960's. Correctional administrators were no less uniformly enthusiastic about reform as a penal purpose."

Viewed in this context the transformations of crime control over the last 40 years can only be perceived as a radical break. However, there is now a growing body of evidence indicating that these arguments may be based on an inaccurate or incomplete assessment of the historical discontinuity between the modern and the late modern penological periods. These new studies, by paying closer attention to the unique developmental trajectories of individual states, challenge the notion that penal modernism and the rehabilitation ideal were uncontested and uniformly implemented throughout the country. Heather Schoenfeld's

---

[1] Rigakos and Hadden (2001) argue that the use of actuarialism in criminal justice dates back to the 1600s, when the emerging English bourgeoisie used it to monitor the social groups that presented a potential threat to its economic ascendancy.

work on Florida's penological history (2014) for example shows that some states (particularly in the South) never fully caught on to the ideas of penal modernism and kept elements of punitiveness from earlier periods. In fact, analyses of prison litigation in Alabama, Georgia, Mississippi, and Arizona suggest that, if anything, punishment in these states was "cheap" and "mean." In Florida, political and bureaucratic arrangements, as well as cultural assumptions about punishment and the capacities of African Americans, undermined penal modernist ideals and practices. Some reforms were implemented, but they never spread to become the dominant, organizing, penological principle against which the punitive turn supposedly took place.

The same broad brush is used to describe the late modern penological era. Scholars have tended to treat the prison boom as a uniform, national phenomenon and to analyze it that way (Lynch 2011). It is true that increases in the use of imprisonment have been pervasive, affecting every state in the nation. However, this approach homogenizes important subnational variations. While all states have seen their prison populations increase, the extent and the rate at which they have changed vary substantially from state to state. In 2009 for example, the incarceration rate was 150 in Maine, but 881 in Louisiana. Similarly, between 1979 and 2009 states saw prison population increases that ranged from 45 percent in Nevada to 744 percent in North Dakota (Mauer 2011). The character of penal sanctioning also varies considerably from state to state; for example, while Arizona reinstated chain gangs, the states of Washington, Oregon and Ohio have quietly adopted policies of de-escalation, the use of community sanctions, and the development of diversion options (Barker 2009). Not only does analyzing aggregated national-level trend data preclude us from understanding how the states have contributed to the incarceration explosion (or not), it is also problematic because it assumes that explanatory factors mean the same thing, and work the same way, across time and space. The evidence at hand shows, however, that states have reacted to the same policy problems (say, rising crime rates) in very different ways, so "to represent our current penal policy predominantly in terms of punitiveness involves a failure to appreciate the diversity and ambiguity of recent government policy" explains Matthews (2005: 190).

This failure to appreciate the complexity of penal policy is also evident in the literature's silence about the role that parole revocations have played in the prison boom. The data suggest that parole revocation has become a major dynamic of prison intake and a salient dimension of the increase in prison population (Petersilia 2003, Simon 1993): over 30 percent of admissions to state and federal prisons are parole violators. Yet scant attention has been paid to this crucial back-end steering mechanism. Lin, Grattet and Petersilia (2010) correctly point out, the significance of back-end sentencing has been largely overlooked in analyses of prison population dynamics. Without an investigation of the factors that drive both front door and back door prison intake, our understanding of the empirical reality of mass incarceration certainly remains incomplete, and perhaps even inaccurate. In particular, by analyzing incarceration rates wholesale scholars have implicitly assumed that parole revocations are being driven by the same factors that explain court commitments at the "front end" of the system. However, as we will see in Chapter 3, while parole has not been immune to the widespread transformation of crime control that has taken place over the last fifty years, it is unclear whether the evolution of parole and the increase in parole revocations can be interpreted through the same punitive lens. In addition, there is no particular reason to believe that the theories developed to explain incarceration should explain parole revocation, as parole is an administrative rather political agency, and parole decisionmaking is somewhat autonomous from the rest of the criminal justice system. As a matter of fact, a cursory examination of correlation coefficients between incarceration rates and parole revocation rates over the 1978-2007 period shows that the relationship between the two can be characterized as weak at best (r=.0453). The coefficients vary greatly in time and space as well[2], which calls into question the extent to which incarceration rates accurately reflect penal sensibilities in a given jurisdiction at a given time, and suggests that the meaning and the use of revocation as a sanction need to be examined more closely and more rigorously.

The reality of American penal sanctioning is therefore much more complicated, profoundly fragmented, and deeply multi-dimensional than the concept of a punitive turn or new penology implies. In the words of Zimring and Hawkins, the "fifty one different countries" that

---

[2] For a more in-depth discussion, see Chapter 3.

make up the American criminal justice system (referring to the state and federal legal systems) may be more akin to "a group of autonomous units functioning independently but marching together" than to "a single organism having diverse organs" (1991: 137). These variations in the use of punishment, both within and between states, have yet to be "fully documented, understood, or explained" (Barker 2009: 4), and they are likely to complicate, but also enrich, the broad theoretical arguments that dominate the criminological literature.

STUDY GOALS AND CONTRIBUTIONS

The purpose of this project is to examine the following questions: Why do some states rely on confinement more than others? Why do incarceration and parole revocation rates vary over time? Are the determinants of front-end sentencing the same as the determinants of back-end sentencing? In addressing these questions, this research monograph has three major (and interrelated) goals. The first is to review and synthesize the extensive prison boom literature in order to build a theoretical framework with which to analyze penal sanctioning in the U.S. states. Research on the American phenomenon of penal overindulgence has identified a number of macro-social and demographic factors such as shifts in crime, political culture, population demographics, sentencing structure, and economic conditions thought to capture salient dimensions of state variation as sources of change in the size of state prison populations. However, these studies tend to offer only rather hollow theorizations of what could arguably be the most salient dimension of all — namely, the state itself. Recent scholarship on the impact of the democratic process on policy-making may help to build better theoretical models to explain the choices states have made regarding the use of large scale imprisonment as a policy tool.

The second goal of this study is to apply this expanded theoretical framework to the analysis of differences in the scope of penal sanctioning in the American states, with a particular focus on examining variation in state incarceration rates and state parole revocation rates over a thirty-year period (1978-2007). To date, no study has analyzed the determinants of back-end sentencing; consequently, the results of these analyses can then be used to suggest whether a separate theoretical model is needed to explain parole revocation.

The third goal is to contribute to the small, but growing, body of literature attempting to provide more thoughtful analyses of the United States' perceived punitiveness: are we as punitive as we think we are? Do contemporary penal practices mean what we think they mean? What can sub-national variations tell us about contemporary penological ideals and practices?

The research presented here makes three distinct contributions to the penology research literature. First, it expands the analytical time frame and broadens the scope of theoretical explanations. Second, it examines how the determinants of sentencing practices have changed over time. Finally, it develops a framework for analyzing variations in state parole revocation rates—the only study to date to attempt to shed some light on this overlooked, yet crucial, criminal justice system steering mechanism.

OVERVIEW OF THE BOOK

Chapter 2 provides a genealogical account of the prison boom. Relying on the very large body of research examining how and why the country embarked on an aggressive program of prison expansion in the 1970s, the chapter teases out the social, political, economic, and cultural forces that were responsible for the build-up in imprisonment and have continued to drive prison populations to historically unprecedented sizes. Studies have investigated penal sanctioning with uneven focus and intensity, leaving some aspects of the processes that contributed to the incarceration explosion theoretically and empirically underdeveloped. Up to this point virtually all researchers have concentrated almost exclusively on "front-end sentences" (offenders sent to prison through court sentences), and have largely ignored back-end sentences (parolees returned to custody). Chapter 3 attempts to fill this gap in our understanding of mass incarceration by unpacking the "black box" of the parole revocation process in order to contextualize the meaning of revocation as a sanction, and to identify salient dimensions upon which a conceptual model of the use of revocation can be constructed.

The analyses set forth in Chapters 5 and 6 are based on an original dataset that contains information on all fifty states for every year in the study period (1978-2007). Chapter 4 describes the data collection techniques employed, the operationalization and measurement of the variables, and the analytic strategy used in this research monograph to investigate the state-level determinants of incarceration rates and parole revocation rates in the U.S. states between 1978 and 2007.

Chapter 5 examines front-end sentencing using negative binomial regression. The analyses replicate and extend prior analyses of the predictors of incarceration rates by elaborating upon and refining prevailing theoretical frameworks. The analytical models also examine whether and how the drivers of imprisonment have varied over time. In Chapter 6 the same analytic and modeling strategy is employed to analyze parole revocation rates. In that chapter it is argued that numerous factors, including those related to crime, symbolic threats, practical constraints, sentencing policies, and the democratic process, are important determinants of penal sanctioning, both at the front end and at the back end. It is also argued that it is important to recognize that the impact of these factors is historically contingent. In addition, the case is made that the ways in which these factors influence front door and back door prison intake are sufficiently different that it is necessary to build analytical models specific to parole revocation.

Chapter 2
A Genealogy of the Prison Boom

In 1973 the National Advisory Commission on Criminal Justice Standards and Goals, charged with evaluating the state of the judicial system, recommended closing down juvenile detention centers and freezing prison construction for a decade. The Commission's recommendations were based on a decade of declining prison populations, as well as the concern that prisons were criminogenic and should therefore be replaced by alternative sentences. In the words of the Commission, "the prison, the reformatory, and the jail have achieved a shocking record of failure. There is overwhelming evidence that these institutions create crime rather than prevent it" (1973: 597). In a sudden and unprecedented development, however, prison populations started growing by leaps and bounds until, at the turn of the twenty-first century, America's jails and prisons held more than two million inmates. If it were a city, the current U.S. carceral system would be the country's fourth largest metropolis (Wacquant 2009: 114).

HOW DID WE GET HERE FROM THERE?

In the span of three short decades, the way in which this country punishes and manages crime was radically transformed. This spectacular turnabout has perplexed scholars and observers, and a large body of empirical research has been devoted to understanding the causes of the country's penchant for penal overindulgence. From a purely descriptive point of view, penologists who study prison growth (Blumstein and Beck 1999, 2005; Raphael and Stoll 2004, 2009; Raphael 2009; Pfaff 2009) have shown that, at the most basic level, the dramatic thirty-year upward trend in incarceration rates (Figure 2.1) was the result of too many people entering prison and staying there too long — what some have called the "iron law of prison populations" (Clear and Austin 2009: 308).

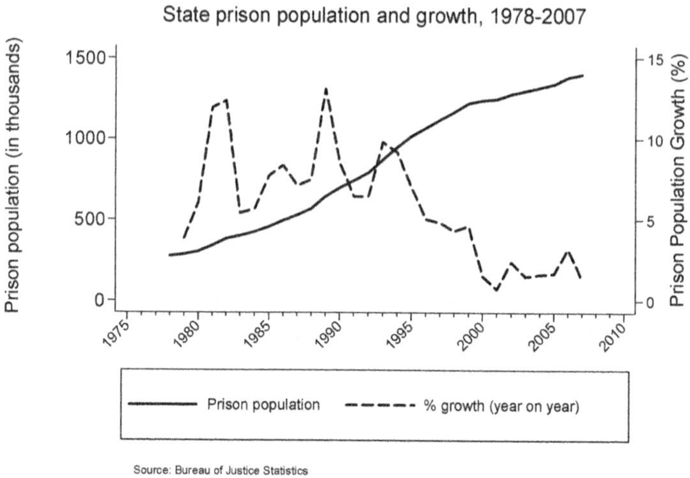

Source: Bureau of Justice Statistics

Figure 2.1 State prison population and annual growth rate, 1978-2007

These studies differ in methods and ways of estimating variables such as time served, but they typically identify the different stages of the criminal justice system that have a significant impact on the prison population — most notably arrests, prison admissions, and length of stay — and endeavor to quantify their respective contributions to prison growth. The most basic of such models of prison growth is the *stock-and-flow* model used by Blumstein and Beck (2005). Blumstein and Beck examined the contribution of three factors – crime rates, prison admission, and time served in prison[3] – to the growth of the prison population in two time periods, 1980 to 1991 and 1991 to 2002. They found that in the early period, (1980-91) prison admissions accounted

---

[3] Expected time served was calculated as the ratio of the total prison stock to the number of new court commitments. This measure includes the probability that a new court commitment will be returned to incarceration and serve additional time for violating the terms of his conditional release.

for the bulk of prison population growth (63 percent), followed by time served (40 percent), and crime rates (22 percent). In the later period (1991-2002), further increases in prison population were driven largely by time served (60 percent), followed by new admissions (40 percent), while crime rates – which were declining through most of the later period – were no longer a factor driving prison growth.

Another approach, used by Raphael and Stoll (2009), relies on a *steady-state* model of the incarceration process that decomposes changes in prison populations into behavioral components (crime), prison admissions, and time served.4 Their study explicitly incorporates the endogenous relationship between crime and incarceration to correct for possible overestimates of the effects of policy responses to crime. Although Raphael and Stoll's approach to decomposing prison growth is different from Blumstein and Beck's, their estimates of the effect of changes in crime rates on changes in the prison population are consistent with those derived by Blumstein and Beck. They find that crime accounts for 17 percent of the prison population growth between 1984 and 2002, while increases in time served and prison admissions explain 35 percent and 48 percent of the total change in incarceration rates, respectively.

Relying on yet a different approach, Pfaff (2009) uses counterfactual analyses to examine the effects of prison admissions and time served on correctional population growth in eleven states over the period 1983-2002. Unlike Raphael and Stoll who computed mean time served from their distribution by assuming expected values for time served for the intervals of their empirical distribution, Pfaff calculates the actual percentiles of the distribution of time served, and reports the median, 75th, and 90th percentiles of the distribution for each state in his sample. This allows him to show that the trends in distribution of time served are comparatively constant over time. He then simulates prison growth, first keeping the level of admissions fixed at an initial year and allowing releases to vary according to their actual patterns, then keeping the release patterns fixed at an initial year and allowing admissions to vary according to their actual patterns. Although the magnitude of the effects is not quantified, his results indicate that changes in admissions account for more of the prison growth than release patterns (which include time served).

---

⁴ By using data from the National Corrections Reporting Program, Raphael and Stoll are able to calculate actual time served rather than having to estimate it.

Collectively, these studies suggest that it is policy factors affecting admissions and time served that are largely responsible for the growth of prison populations during the last two decades of the twentieth century. By further breaking down their analysis into two time periods, Blumstein and Beck are also able to demonstrate that the components of the growth changed in the 1990s. In their study the influence of crime rates disappeared and the role of admissions decreased, while time served accounted for a greater share of the growth. These shifts coincided with the end of the era of major sentencing reforms,[5] and a marked decrease in the rate of prison growth. Figure 2.1 shows, in this regard, that annual growth rates peaked at 13% in the early 1990s, and have been declining consistently since the mid-1990s to settle at less than 2% in recent years. In-keeping with the slowing in the growth of prison populations, the number of offenders in state prisons and the incarceration rate of state prisoners have started to diverge, with a leveling off in the incarceration rate taking place during the 2000s (Figure 2.2). This suggests that prison populations are now roughly keeping pace with the rate of growth of the U.S. resident population.

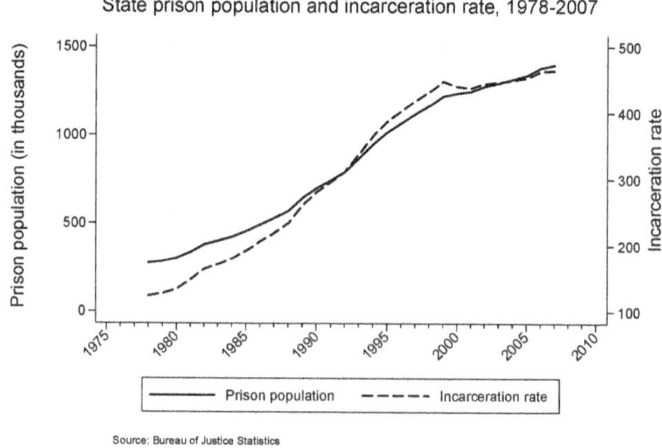

Figure 2.2 State prison population and incarceration rate, 1978-2007

---

[5] By 1996, the sentencing reform movement was over in most states (Stemen 2005).

The sentencing reform movement that swept through the U.S. introduced a now well-known panoply of policies — including various forms of structured or guideline-based sentencing practices, minimum sentencing requirements, truth-in-sentencing reforms (mandating that offenders serve at least 70, 85 or, in some cases/states, 100 percent of the sentence imposed by the court), violent offender provisions, and habitual offender laws (also known as "three strikes" laws). These legislatively enacted policies changed how court sentences where handed down at the "front end" of the system, while also curtailing or reducing parole boards' authority to make release decisions at the "back end." Between 1975 and 2002, 19 states abolished discretionary parole, nine states adopted presumptive sentencing systems, and 17 instituted some form of sentencing guidelines. These actions resulted in different combinations of determinate/indeterminate and structured/unstructured sentencing systems, and led to the creation of a patchwork of sentencing practices across the country (Table 2.1).

Table 2-1 Determinate and structured sentencing in the states, 2002

State	Determinacy		Structure		
	No parole	Parole	Presumptive sentencing	Presumptive guidelines	Voluntary guidelines
Alabama		♦			
Alaska		♦	♦		
Arizona	♦		♦		
Arkansas		♦			♦
California	♦		♦		
Colorado		♦	♦		
Connecticut		♦			
Delaware	♦				♦
Florida	♦			♦	
Georgia		♦			
Hawaii		♦			
Idaho		♦			
Illinois	♦				
Indiana	♦		♦		
Iowa		♦			
Kansas	♦			♦	
Kentucky		♦			

Table 2-2 Determinate and structured sentencing in the states, 2002 (Cond't)

State	Determinacy			Structure	
	No parole	Parole	Presumptive sentencing	Presumptive guidelines	Voluntary guidelines
Louisiana		♦			♦
Maine	♦				
Maryland		♦			♦
Massachusetts		♦			
Michigan		♦		♦	
Minnesota	♦			♦	
Mississippi	♦				
Missouri		♦			♦
Montana		♦			
Nebraska		♦			
Nevada		♦			
New Hampshire		♦			
New Jersey		♦	♦		
New Mexico	♦		♦		
New York		♦			
North Carolina	♦			♦	
North Dakota		♦			
Ohio	♦		♦		
Oklahoma		♦			
Oregon	♦			♦	
Pennsylvania		♦		♦	
Rhode Island		♦	♦		
South Carolina		♦			
South Dakota		♦			
Tennessee		♦		♦	
Texas		♦			
Utah		♦			♦
Vermont		♦			
Virginia	♦				♦
Washington	♦			♦	
West Virginia		♦			
Wisconsin	♦				♦
Wyoming		♦			

Source: Stemen (2005)

The implementation of these policies marked a significant change in the sentencing system under which the country had been operating for close to a hundred years. Until the early 1970s, the U.S. operated under an indeterminate sentencing model that was organized around the twin goals of individualization and rehabilitation. It was believed that rehabilitation could be achieved by tailoring punishment based on the unique characteristics of the offender. Consequently, states set few restrictions on judges' discretion to impose specific sanctions or sentences of a particular length, and parole boards had broad authority to release offenders when they deemed it appropriate (Frase 1991; Griset 1991; Reitz 2001; Rothman 1983; Tonry 1997). The cornerstone of the system, judicial discretion, came under sustained attack in the 1970s; for some, it resulted in sentences that were considered too lenient or too short. Others were concerned about the potential for abuse and discrimination. One point that many critics agreed on was that sentencing should be more structured and more determinate (Bales 2010). Criticized by both progressives and conservatives, the penal welfare framework gave way in the 1970s to a system based on retributive ideals and featuring rather punitive sanctions.

Striking changes to sentencing and parole policies followed as the states and the federal system sought to remove variability and arbitrariness and restore fairness to sentencing and release decisions. As the data featured in figure 2.3 indicate, states accomplished this goal

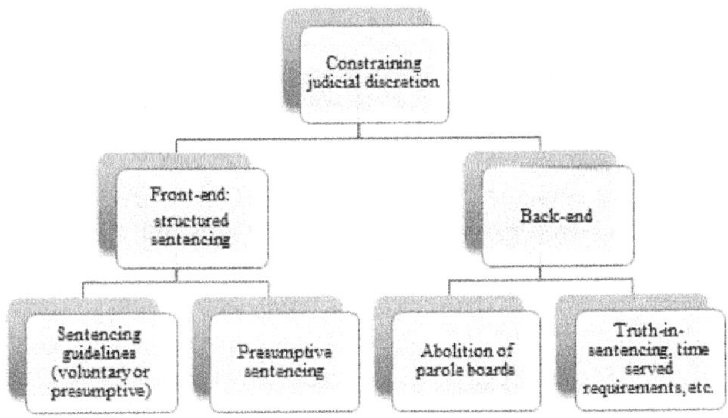

Figure 2.3 Reforms constraining judicial discretion at the front- and back-ends of state sentencing systems

by constraining judicial discretion through the implementation of structured sentencing, and/or shifting the locus of discretion by eliminating or limiting parole boards' authority; the former controls sentencing decisions and the length of the prison terms imposed at the front end, while the latter controls releases and time served at the back end. Specifically, at the front end, states introduced structure into their sentencing systems through one of two similar, yet distinct, mechanisms (Stemen 2005).

The first, <u>presumptive sentencing</u> is a system of single recommended prison terms or narrow sentence ranges within the wider statutory sentence range *for each offense or offense class*. It is termed "presumptive" because it is presumed that the judge will impose the recommended prison term or a term from within the narrow recommended range. The second mechanism, <u>sentencing guidelines</u>, is a system of multiple recommended sentences and dispositions, and a set of procedures designed to guide judicial sentencing decisions and sentencing outcomes, and to ensure that all offenders committing similar offenses and with similar criminal histories receive similar sentences. Under sentencing guidelines, each offense or offense class will have multiple sentence recommendations based on the prior criminal history of the offender, and recommended prison terms are generally determined according to the severity of the offense committed *and* the prior criminal history of the offender.[6] Sentencing guidelines can be either presumptive or voluntary, depending on the degree to which states use formal legal authority to constrain judicial sentencing decisions.

At the back end, states moved toward determinate sentencing systems — i.e., systems *without* discretionary parole release as a mechanism for releasing offenders from prison (Reitz and Reitz 1993; Stemen 2005; Tonry 1987). Without discretionary parole release, offenders are automatically released from prison after serving a statutorily-determined portion of the term imposed (e.g., 85 percent of their sentence). The "determinacy" in the system refers to the effort to ensure that time served by offenders is primarily determined by the

---

[6] This differs from presumptive sentencing systems, where recommended sentences are determined entirely by the severity of the current offense.

length of the sentence imposed by the judge rather than by the discretionary release decision-making of the parole board.

Scholars have not yet come to a consensus about the precise impact of these sentencing reforms on prison admissions and time served,[7] but they have suspected that sentencing reforms may affect incarceration rates by shifting the locus of sentencing discretion and power from the judiciary (judges and parole boards) to the executive (prosecutors) and the legislative branches. This "hydraulic displacement of discretion" (McCoy 1984; Tonry and Coffee 1987) has been hypothesized to give more power to prosecutors to coerce defendants into taking guilty pleas, and to mask the very sentencing disparities that structured sentencing was designed to eliminate (Rathke 1982; Savelsberg 1994; Ulmer 1996).[8] This theory, while popular, has received rather limited empirical attention. However, in their studies of case dispositions before and after the implementation of guidelines in Minnesota and Ohio, respectively, Miethe (1987) and Wooldredge and Griffin (2005) found in their separate studies that sentencing reforms did <u>not</u>, in fact, result in harsher sentencing decisions or greater disparities in case disposition. It should be noted, however, that Wooldredge and Griffin also point out that their data showed considerable differences in disposition rates across the 24 jurisdictions they examined. The impact of the displacement of discretion might be more readily apparent when looking at parole revocations since the abolition of parole boards (or the curtailment of their authority) was aimed precisely at restricting discretion in an effort to ensure that offenders were not "let off too easy," but this hypothesis has yet to be empirically tested.

The extent to which the hydraulic displacement of discretion affects incarceration rates remains unclear then. Neither do we

---

[7] Early studies of guidelines and determinate sentencing laws suffered from methodological shortcomings that hindered researchers' ability to parse the role of sentencing policies in the dynamics of prison population change and separate the impacts of sentencing policies from long-term trends in corrections (Casper and Brereton 1984; Hewitt and Clear 1983; Kautt and Delone 2006; Lipson and Peterson 1980).

[8] Ulmer and Kramer, for example, show that loose guidelines provide a "menu of sentencing options" (1998: 403) with windows of discretion that allow decision-makers to use substantive rationality and extralegal factors to adapt sentencing decisions to the specific characteristics of the local context.

understand the precise mechanisms through which this displacement may happen. What the research investigating sentencing reforms does show, however, is that the direction and magnitude of the effects of the new sentencing policies may depend on three specific factors. The first, and perhaps most obvious, is that different types of policies have different impacts: Stemen and his colleagues (2005) found that mandatory sentencing laws, three strikes laws, and the creation and enforcement of drug laws had a significant, positive effect on incarceration rates, but their results did not support the argument that time served requirements (such as truth-in-sentencing laws) are associated with higher incarceration rates.

Second, sentencing policies may have a different effect depending on whether they were adopted with the intention of being "tough on crime" or of curbing the run-away growth of prison populations and corrections budgets. For example, Marvell's (1995) longitudinal study of sentencing guidelines in nine states between 1974 and 1993 determined that guidelines had a moderating effect on incarceration rates in states where the guidelines were tied to legislative directives to consider prison capacity and correctional resources. He also found that guidelines did not have a significant impact on admission rates. In a subsequent study Marvell and Moody (1996) showed that determinate sentencing laws were associated with prison growth and increased court commitments in only two of the 10 states they examined (Indiana and California), but reduced populations in the others. They conclude that the direction (positive or negative) of the effect of determinate sentencing laws on correctional populations hinged upon policymakers' framing of the laws as either "tough on crime" measures or prison population reduction measures. Their findings support Kramer's (1992) analysis of the implementation of guidelines in Pennsylvania. Kramer shows that the state adopted guidelines as part of a sentencing scheme designed to produce more commitments, longer sentences, and higher incarceration rates, and they were indeed associated with an increase in the latter. In contrast, in states such as Minnesota, Washington, and Oregon, where guidelines were explicitly linked with capacity and correctional resources, prison population sizes leveled off or decreased (Alschuler 1991; Frase 1995; Tonry 1991, 1996). Nicholson-Crotty (2004), in a pooled time-series analysis of the impact of guidelines in the 50 states between 1975 and 1998, came to a similar conclusion. His findings show a relationship between mandatory guidelines and increased commitment and incarceration rates in states where sentencing decisions are *not* linked to capacity and expenditures. Where they are resource-driven, the impact on prison populations is either negative or insignificant.

Finally, the impact of sentencing reforms may be tied to the combined effects of policies, as Stemen's (2005) findings suggest. His results show that the combination of determinate sentencing and *presumptive* sentencing guidelines resulted in lower incarceration rates and smaller prison population growth. This outcome was not present in states with determinate sentencing and *voluntary* sentencing guidelines; in these states, incarceration rates were higher and prison population growth was greater than in other states.

Although the research that is necessary to get a firmer grasp of the effects of sentencing policies on state prison populations is just starting to emerge in the literature, the new policies that were put in place in the 1980s and 1990s played a significant role in the growth of the carceral system; that much seems clear. But what "tangle of transformative forces" (Garland 2001: 2) paved the way for the adoption of these new policies? Why did our response to crime take the form that it did, when it did?

THE PATH OF LEAST RESISTANCE

In his insightful book *The Culture of Control* (2001), David Garland argues that: "to investigate the new patterns of crime control is [...] to investigate the remaking of society and its institutions for the production of order" (6). The complex historical processes that took us from a welfare state in the early 1970s to a full-blown penal state in a mere thirty years later defy simplification, as the path diagram in Figure 2.4 demonstrates; the various factors associated with changes in the size and growth of prison populations coexist in messy, sometimes contradictory, relationships. Any attempt to weave them together into an account of our contemporary practices of crime and punishment necessarily imposes an artificial and perhaps misleading organization and coherence upon a confusing, spatially-differentiated, multi-dimensional historical process. It is, however, a place from which the analysis can begin.

Scholars have drawn particular attention to two sets of transformative forces that helped to facilitate the introduction of a law-

and-order regime and the re-invention of the classic prison. The first set of forces consists of social and economic changes that eroded the foundations of New Deal liberalism in the period of the 1960-1970s. These changes in turn resulted in major political and cultural realignments that formed the public policy formation terrain upon which crime control policies were built and prison expansion took off in the following two decades.

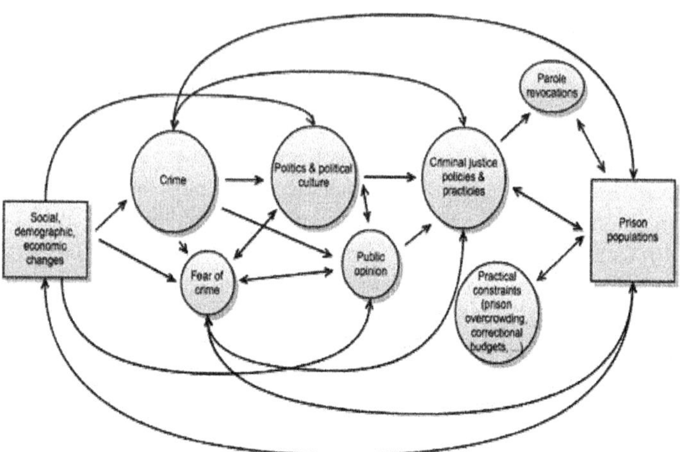

Figure 2.4 Conceptual diagram of the main factors influencing the size and growth of prison populations in the U.S.

The crisis of New Deal Liberalism

The post-World War II political order was characterized by two decades of peace and stability, sustained economic growth, political optimism, and progressivism that raised expectations about the role of government in managing economic life and guaranteeing the wellbeing and prosperity of its population. The rising standards of living funded a "politics of solidarity" and a strategy of welfarist governance in which the state provided social services, health care, education, housing, and unemployment benefits for its citizens. This commitment to social democracy extended to the penal realm, where the rehabilitative model promoted progressive penal policies based upon the individualized treatment of offenders (Garland 2001; Reitz 2001; Simon 2007). Rehabilitation of criminals was viewed as possible, and their reintegration into society, desirable, and penal welfarism sought to achieve these goals through professional treatment, education, and social work support (Garland 2001). This mode of governance was destabilized and eventually collapsed, however, as demographic changes, the social crises of the 1960-70s (urban race riots, violent civil rights struggles, anti-war demonstrations, and political assassinations), and deteriorating economic conditions in the 1970s made U.S. society more crime-prone, eroded confidence in the welfarist framework, and brought about a governmental crisis.

Figure 2.5 U.S. crime rates (per 100,000 population), 1960-2012

Crime rates rose sharply across all major offense categories (including property crimes) in the 1960s and 1970s. As the data displayed in Figure 2.5 indicate, property and violent crime rates roughly tripled in twenty years, and continued to climb until the early to mid-1990s when they reached their peak and proceeded to fall as steeply as they had gone up. Scholars have linked the sustained increase in crime in the 1960-70s to a number of socio-demographic and cultural changes that, in combination: increased opportunities for crime (higher standards of living and mass consumption meant that the new targets for theft in the form of high value, portable goods, appeared on the market); reduced situational controls (women entered the workforce, and people moved out of densely populated neighborhoods and into sprawling suburban subdivisions); increased the size of the population most prone to criminal behavior (a large cohort of young males came of age); and relaxed informal social control and social norms (Bottom and Wiles 1995; Felson and Cohen 1980; Garland 2001; LaFree 1998).

Since punishment is a direct response to crime, one would expect more crime to result in higher incarceration rates—especially when increases in crime rates (both violent and property crime — Figure 2.5) are as substantial and as sustained as they were in the U.S. from the 1960s through the mid-1990s. This functionalist argument is supported by some of the research that shows a positive, significant relationship between crime rates and incarceration rates (Langan 1991; Ouimet and Tremblay 1996; Sykes, Vito and McElrath 1987). Researchers have struggled to quantify accurately the degree to which increases in crime translate into prison growth, however, because the relationship between crime and incarceration is notoriously complex: more crime may lead to higher incarceration rates, but mass incarceration and incapacitation of repeat offenders may deter crime. Failure to appropriately control for the feedback loop created by the reciprocal relationship between crime rates and prison population growth (i.e., treating crime as an exogenous variable in regression models of incarceration rates) leads to biased estimates (Listokin 2003; Pfaff 2007). Unfortunately, addressing endogeneity is quite challenging, and very few studies do so convincingly.[9]

Moreover, as Figure 2.6 demonstrates, the effect of crime on incarceration is not as intuitive, straightforward, or mechanical as this

---

[9] In his meta-analysis of the prison boom literature, Pfaff argues that Listokin's (2003) is the only study that explicitly and convincingly controls for the endogenous relationship. He does so by using abortion as an instrument for crime. His results show a doubling of the magnitude of crime's effect on prison admissions.

functionalist argument would suggest, which would also explain why tests of this relationship often produce only mixed results.

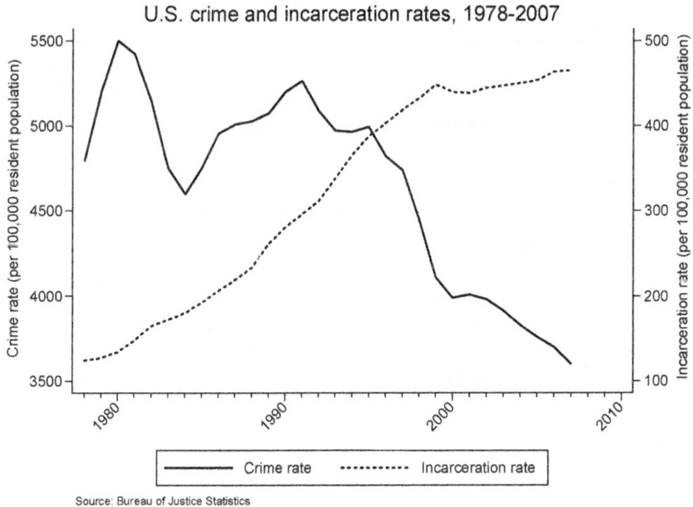

Figure 2.6 U.S. crime and incarceration rates, 1978-2007

More significantly perhaps, the "crime problem" became the solution to the crisis of the New Deal political order (Simon 2007). The social instability brought about by rising crime, deteriorating race relations, anti-war demonstrations, and civil rights struggles in the 1960s and 70s, not only generated anxiety among the American public about the decline of civility, but also contributed to a broad social malaise about seemingly intractable social and economic problems (inflation, unemployment, the collapse of industrial production, and the increasing precariousness of the labor market) that the post-war political order appeared relatively powerless to address and resolve (Scheingold 1991, 1995). As a result many people, especially in the middle-class, started to question the legitimacy and effectiveness of welfare institutions that appeared to be disproportionately benefitting undeserving and dangerous segments of the population. As economic conditions worsened with the 1973 oil crisis and the country entered into a recession, the middle-class grew more resentful, and more reluctant to support expensive welfare policies that they deemed at odds with their own economic interests (Garland 2001). This governmental crisis gave politicians competing for support powerful incentives to reframe anxieties about social and economic problems while lowering expectations about what the government could and should do to address these issues. Of the various programs around which they could rally (environmentalism, the expansion of social insurance programs, the civil rights movement), crime offered the least political or legal resistance to governmental action (Garland 2001; Scheingold 1991; Simon 2007).

For political elites to use crime and punishment in response to social and economic problems is hardly without historical precedent. One of the basic functions of the State is to guarantee social order, and the power to punish its citizens is a fundamental component of its authority (Foucault 1977; Garland 1990; Jacobs and Carmichael 2001). When faced with what Garland calls "a Marxist problem of order" stemming from the social and political instability caused by class antagonisms and precarious labor market conditions,[10] states have used penal sanctioning as a way to "manage the underclass" and preserve established structures of power and privilege (Adamson 1984; Chambliss 1994; Foucault 1995; Garland 1990; Savelsberg 1994). For example, Rusche and Kirchheimer (1939) showed that transformations in European penal systems (and the rise of imprisonment more specifically) between the 16th and 19th century corresponded to phases of economic development and changes in the labor market. Michael Ignatieff (1978) and David Rothman (1990) further elaborated on this

---

[10] In the Marxist view, the capitalist system creates problem populations that must be controlled in order to preserve social relations of production. Marx noted that capitalist accumulation "constantly produces a population which is superfluous to capital's average requirements for its own valorization, and is therefore a surplus population," a "disposable industrial reserve army" (1977:782). During good economic times, this surplus labor serves to keep employed workers' wages down and maintain profits for the ruling class. During downward swings in the industrial cycle, however, a criminal underclass culled from surplus labor can arise—a potential political threat and an economic drain on the resources of the state. Punishment is therefore seen as reflecting both crime- and class-control objectives that are themselves linked to the larger economic context.

theory, arguing that as capitalism weakened traditional forms of control, it came to rely on the prison to establish social stability. Economic threat theory has been criticized for economic reductionism and historical revisionism (Garland 1990), as well as for its implicit assumption of coordinated social control. Nevertheless, that theory quite properly draws our attention to the importance of economic conditions as a driver of prison population growth.

Notwithstanding the conceptual limitations of economic threat theory, there is some empirical support for the theory. In their meta-analysis, Chiricos and Delone (1992) show that 60 percent of the 147 studies they examined reported that states with worse economic conditions (measured through the unemployment rate, for instance) are associated with higher incarceration rates (Cappell and Sykes 1991; Chiricos and Delone 1992; Greenberg 1977; Greenberg and West 2001; Jacobs and Carmichael 2001; Lessan 1991; Western 2006). However, it is difficult to draw solid conclusions from these findings because the magnitude of estimates varies a great deal between studies, and appear to be sensitive to small changes in model specification; for example, when Greenberg and West add unemployment-year interaction terms to their model the effect of the unemployment rate changes direction (it becomes negative), and loses its statistical significance. Studies using measures of economic inequality (Gini coefficient, poverty rate, or average personal income) to predict incarceration rates yield similarly erratic findings. A non-linear relationship between economic threat and punitive sanctions may account for these inconsistent results, but even the stronger studies of the drivers of the prison boom ignore this possibility.

Rightward drift

Politically, crime provided an important wedge to construct a new political order. With the decline of Jim Crow Laws and the enactment of the Civil Rights Act of 1964, conservative politicians needed to retreat from explicit support for legal racial segregation and rebuild themselves around a more race-neutral agenda. They found this agenda in the themes of the Goldwater campaign of 1964 — namely, anti-communism, states' rights, mistrust of New Deal-style government, public morality, and fighting crime (Alexander 2010; Beckett 1997). The burgeoning *Republican Southern strategy* exploited racial fears and antagonisms and mobilized the resentment of white working-class voters who were most directly affected by racial integration measures and racial equality laws:

> "[They] were suddenly forced to compete on equal terms with Blacks for jobs and status and [they] lived in neighborhoods adjoining Black ghettos. Their children ... attended schools most likely to fall under busing orders" (Alexander 2010: 46; Edsall and Edsall 1992).

This (often racialized) political rhetoric shaped the nature and direction of debates about crime, and eventually gave rise to the nation's repressive crime control policies (Beckett 1997; Erikson, Wright and McIver 1989; Scheingold 1998; Wacquant 2005).

The Republican Party — long considered the party of "law and order" — proved particularly adept at exploiting fears of crime and widespread social insecurities and setting off the contemporary thrust of "governing through crime" (Simon 2007). It is not surprising, then, that studies tend to find that a strong Republican Party is associated with increased corrections spending (Caldeira and Cowart 1980; Caldeira 1983; Stucky et al. 2007), higher incarceration rates (Jacobs and Carmichael 2001; Stemen 2005; Western 2006), and faster prison population growth (Jacobs and Helms 1999). This is not to say that Democrats have defended liberal positions on crime — far from it. Responding to the same public pressures to be "tough on crime," and in an effort to wrest control of the crime and drug issues from Republicans, Democrats, too, have backed strong crime control measures (Alexander 2010; Finckenauer 1978).

Law and order policies became "sacred pillars of state government," as Schoenfeld's interview with a Democratic Florida legislator illustrates:

> "[legislative enhancements] put legislators in a very difficult position. Because mandatory sentences on their face look very good. Are you against a strong criminal justice system? You can't [be]. That's like being against American apple pie" (quoted in Campbell and Schoenfeld 2013: 1408).

Similarly, when seeking the Presidency, Bill Clinton highlighted his record of being tough on crime as Governor of Arkansas — which included the execution of a mentally-impaired man (Ricky Ray) — boasting, "I can be nicked a lot, but no one can say that I'm soft on crime" (quoted in Alexander 2010:56). He went on to work on the passage of some of the toughest sentencing laws and preside over the largest increases in state and federal prison populations of any president in American history. As a result of these changes in the political culture, then, the crime policy-making process became highly politicized — though some have suggested that one would expect partisan differences and the influence of the Republican Party on crime policy to become less significant over time as politicians from both parties compete to be seen as punitive and unforgiving in the treatment of offenders (Beckett and Sasson 2000; Greenberg and West 2001). This hypothesis has yet to be rigorously tested.

The question of how Republican strength leads to higher incarceration rates and faster prison growth remains fairly open. One of the ways in which increased Republican political strength in the states may have fed the prison boom is through the vast redirecting of resources toward the criminal justice system. Corrections spending grew 350 percent in the 1980s and 1990s — or an increase from 1.6 to 3 percent of total state expenditures (Maguire and Pastore 2002). By 2005, the states were spending $43 billion per year on corrections (Pfaff 2008). Studies show that Republican presidential administrations devoted more resources to corrections and other criminal justice programs compared to Democratic administrations (Caldeira and Cowart 1980), and that increases in Republican strength are associated with increases in corrections spending (Jacobs and Helms 1999) or capital spending on prisons (Spelman 2009) Spelman also reports a positive relationship between prison capital spending and prison population growth, but this finding is problematic because the relationship may be endogenous — i.e., more spending on corrections may lead to more prisoners, but more prisoners may lead to more spending on corrections.

There is little systematic research examining whether greater Republican strength in the states produces more severe penal sanctions or an escalation in the punishments stipulated by law for specific criminal acts, but studies conducted by Dyke (2003) and Huber and Gordon (2004) suggest that prosecutors (Dyke) and judges (Huber and Gordon) were more punitive in years when they faced elections;

prosecutors dismissed fewer charges, and judges were more likely to favor prison sentences over alternative sentences (fines, probation) and to sentence defendants to longer terms. These findings may reflect the need to attract voters with tough-on-crime stances, especially in Republican-dominated states.

But perhaps the most important way in which partisan politics influenced the expansion of the penal system is through the covert emphasis on race in the law-and-order rhetoric that came to dominate political discourse in the 1980s and 1990s. Racial threat theory contends that when a large or expanding minority group begins to threaten a dominant group's position, power, or access to resources, sharp reactions to such threats can be expected (Blumer 1980; Bobo 1999; Bobo and Hutchings 1996) in the form of mechanisms of competitive exclusion (Barth 1969; King et al. 2012; Olzak and Shanahan 2014). These mechanisms include severe punitive measures that (at least indirectly) target minorities, restrict the threat of a growing Black population, and maintain a social distance between middle-class Whites and underclass Blacks. Examining the recent history of racial relations in the U.S., Loic Wacquant argues that this form of racialized social control is the latest in a long series of institutions designed to dominate minorities. In this regard he observes: "the prison in the era of the jobless ghetto functions to warehouse a population made superfluous by urban deindustrialization, but radicalized by the social movements of the 1960s" (Western 2006:56, summarizing Wacquant's argument). Following a similar line of argument, in her book *The New Jim Crow* (2010) Michelle Alexander provides some evidence for this claim. She describes how supposedly colorblind policies such as the War on Drugs are recreating many of the conditions of Jim Crow and perpetuating a "black undercaste" characterized by what Wacquant terms "a closed circuit of perpetual marginality" (2000).

There is considerable support for these arguments in the empirical literature. Minorities have undoubtedly borne the brunt of the prison boom — especially young Black and Hispanic males who are vastly overrepresented in correctional populations (Neal and Rick 2014). In part, this is due to the racial differences in the crimes that can be expected to lead to imprisonment (Bridges and Crutchfield 1988). For example, as Keen and Jacobs (2009) point out, between 1983-1999 the mean Black violent crime arrest rate was 7.7 higher than the same rate for Whites. However, a number of studies suggest that this cannot be the only explanation for the racial prison admission ratios, and that one must examine the disparate racial impacts of colorblind sentencing policies (Schlesinger 2011; Tonry 1995). [11] A large body of research confirms a positive, significant relationship between the size (and, sometimes, the growth) of Black populations and nearly every aspect of the criminal justice system, ranging from fear of crime (Britt 2000; Spohn and Holleran 2000; Spohn 2000; Steffensmeier and Demuth 2000), to police strength (Huff and Stahura 2006; Jackson and Carroll 1981; Liska et al. 1981), corrections spending (Jacobs and Helms 1999; Stucky et al. 2007), sentencing severity (Ulmer and Johnson 2004), incarceration rates (Greenberg and West 2001; Marvell and Moody 1996; Nicholson-Crotty 2004; Sorenson and Stemen 2002), and the use of the death penalty (Jacobs et al. 2007).

More recently, a few studies have suggested that the relationship between African American presence and severe criminal justice outcomes may not be a linear one, however. Keen and Jacobs (2009), for example, find an inverted U-shaped relationship between the size of Black populations and racial disparities in imprisonment. They hypothesize in this regard that "growth in African-American proportions beyond ... a threshold can be expected to give this racial minority enough potential votes to weaken policies that lead to higher African-American incarceration rates relative to Whites" (215).

Interestingly, tests of the minority threat hypothesis yield different results for Latinos; with the exception of Stemen (2005), most studies find no relationship between the size of Hispanic populations and incarceration rates. There are several possible reasons for these unexpected findings. As Fox and Guglielmo (2012: 336) explain, in the late nineteenth- and early twentieth-century racial boundaries became predicated on skin pigmentation, placing some groups squarely in one racial category while others, such as foreign-born Whites or Mexican Americans, whose ethnic distinctions are sometimes less visible, often straddle categories. With increasing clarity of ethnic boundaries comes increasing ethnic competition and threat (Barth 1969; Olzak and Shanahan 2014). Alternatively, or perhaps as part of this process, it may be that African-Americans are singled out as an exceptionally

---

[11] For instance in her recently published analysis of mandatory terms and sentencing enhancements Traci Schlesinger (2011) finds that these policies increase overall prison admission rates, but the effects are larger for black men.

threatening racial group because of the social construction of blackness as synonymous with criminality and racial inferiority in the U.S. (Dixon 2006a/b; Muhammad 2010). But it may also be that the relationship is historically contingent; while Latinos were but a small percentage of the U.S. population in 1980, they have recently passed African-Americans as the largest U.S. minority group. As one of the fastest growing demographic, they may become more "threatening" as time passes and their visibility increases. Studies conducted earlier, or focusing on earlier periods, would not have been able to show this impact. In addition, Latino populations tend to be concentrated in certain states/regions; the impact of their numbers would be diluted in aggregate analyses. Whatever the actual reason, the possible differential, time-varying, impact of Black and Hispanic populations on state punitive reactions clearly merits further exploration.

The rightward political drift was accompanied by a substantial cultural realignment that may have contributed to the prison boom as well. One aspect of this realignment is that, as fear of crime acquired new salience, so did the weight of public opinion and citizen ideology in the policy-making process, independent of the influence of partisan politics. Based on the premise that conservatives tend to be more punitive than liberals (Van Dijk and Steinmetz 1988), a few studies have explored whether citizen ideology is associated with harsher crime control measures. Findings have positively linked conservative ideology with incarceration rates (Greenberg and West 2001; Griset 1999; Jacobs and Carmichael 2001; Jacobs and Helms 2001; Sorenson and Stemen 2002; Vaughn 1993), sentence length (Bowers and Waltman 1993), and sanction severity (Tyler and Boeckmann 1997). Jacobs and Helms (1996) also demonstrated that the adoption and implementation of determinate sentencing can be explained by changes in ideology. These findings are consistent with Enns' more recently articulated argument (2014) that public opinion has been a crucial determinant of changes in the country's incarceration rate over the past six decades. Using a measure of public punitiveness he generated from 33 survey questions from three sources (Roper Center Public Opinion Archives, American National Election Study, and General Social Survey), Enns showed that, controlling for crime rate, illegal drug use, inequality, and the party in power, increasing public punitiveness in the post-WWII era was instrumental in not only launching the prison boom, but sustaining it. Enns also found that shifts in the public's punitiveness appear to precede, rather than follow, shifts in congressional attention to crime.

A second factor in this cultural realignment was a shift toward the exclusionary (Young 1999), exemplified by — but not limited to — higher levels of imprisonment. This shift toward the exclusionary is related to both the political rhetoric of law and order and the country's growing ideological conservatism. Taken together, these elements helped critics of the welfare state reject the view of criminals as poorly socialized or maladjusted individuals, and put forward instead the volunteeristic view that, in the words of former British Prime Minister John Major, "crime is a decision, not a disease" (quoted in Garland 2001:191). It became morally legitimate, then, to curtail welfare benefits and education spending, historically used as an informal system of social control, and rely on the formal system of corrections for social control instead (Beckett and Western 2001; Colvin 1990; Garland 1985; Greenberg and West 2001; Piven and Cloward 1972). Scholars have shown that indeed there appears to be a relationship between welfare and imprisonment. Sutton (2000) and Greenberg (1999), for example, show in cross-national studies that countries that provide greater welfare benefits tend to be more reluctant to use incarceration compared to other countries. Beckett and Western (2001) demonstrate a similar relationship in the U.S.

DIFFERENT STATES, DIFFERENT CHOICES?

Stateless state variation

Early studies of the determinants of the prison boom used aggregate national data and therefore treated these processes as a relatively uniform, national-level phenomenon. As recognition of the need to take into account state-specific developments emerged in more recent research, a number of scholars have demonstrated the complex, temporally- and spatially-specific nature of penal policymaking (Barker 2006; Beckett and Western 2001; Gilmore 2007; Gottschalk 2006; Lynch 2010; Savelsberg 1994; Whitman 2003). Their analyses suggest that attention to state and regional differences provides a useful framework for understanding variations in the scope of penal sanctioning among the states, while also offering valuable insights into the underpinnings of the contemporary use of punishment.

These efforts to analyze state variation remain, however, surprisingly "stateless" in nature. Studies have identified a number of macro-social and demographic factors thought to capture salient dimensions of state variation, but they offer rather hollow theorizations of what could arguably be the most salient dimension of all — namely, the state itself. States have not pursued the same kinds of policies in response to the same kinds of policy problems. Faced with similar conditions, state punitive efforts have followed different paths and patterns that we may not be able to fully understand without bringing the state back into our analyses. However, with the exception of Barker (2006, 2009) few scholars (especially in the quantitative literature) have attempted to unpack the essential properties of this variable that plays a central role in much comparative historical research (Skocpol and Amenta 1986; Weir, Orloff, and Skocpol 1988), conceptualize its role in penality, and model how state-specific patterns of governance may have created the patchwork of punishment practices that we see in the U.S. today.

Neo-Marxian scholars, for instance, treat the state as largely epiphenomenal. Like other aspects of society, the state simply reflects existing social relations and the needs of the capitalist economy to preserve the relations of production. Its purpose, therefore, is one of social control and, if necessary, repression. As discussed earlier, this perspective has been criticized for presenting an overly structural and economically over-determined view of the state. By conceptualizing the state as emerging from social interaction, Foucault (1995) offers a more complex view that brings attention to the insidious ways in which state power shapes, regulates, manages (and represses, when necessary) all aspects of social relations. State power at once socializes and controls, constructs its subjects and subjugates them, in a dispersion of power through practices, institutions, and interactions that renders the state almost invisible. Because Foucault rejects the idea that power is a thing that is "held" by someone, his view of the state is devoid of agents and makes no mention of the ideological struggles that shape policy decisions. His theorization therefore reduces the state to a "bare technological scaffolding" (Garland 1990:171), and the pure, disembodied, exercise of power. The same criticism could be leveled against Wacquant's thesis (2004, 2009) that the neoliberal "wedding of social and penal policy at the bottom of the polarized class structure"

(2009: 304) has resulted in the "normalization of insecurity": while Wacquant provides ample evidence of what the convergence of workfare and prisonfare *does*, as Schoenfeld rightfully points out, his account is devoid of "specificity about *whom* or *what* is producing these trends" (2011: 474). There are actors, but they lack agency and are reduced to positions within the neoliberal regime; tellingly, the building of the penal state is described in the passive voice:

> "Now, to turn the penal apparatus into an organizational contraption suitable for curbing and containing social disorders [...] required two transformations. First its processing and warehousing capacities had to be vastly expanded. Second, it had to be remade into a flexible, muscular, and efficacious instrument for the tracking and confinement of [...] troublesome persons" (2009: 65).

These perspectives are valuable and theoretically interesting, but they offer conceptualizations of the state that are difficult, if not impossible, to operationalize. Unfortunately, pluralistic approaches are no more helpful in this respect. According to this view, it is the actions of politicians, individuals, and interest groups that take center-stage; the state becomes merely the backdrop for their conflict-oriented activities. Besides under-theorizing the state, this once prominent perspective in political science ignores the fact that actors must contend with bureaucratic and structural institutional arrangements.

Bringing the state back in

The institutionalist view offers a more theoretically promising and fruitful way to treat the state, which is seen in the Weberian tradition as a highly complex organization made up of "a set of multiple and overlapping institutions invested with administrative, legal, extractive, and coercive powers" (Barker 2009: 30). While it runs the risk of reducing the state to an administrative structure with greater or lesser capacity, and reducing institutions to collections of bureaucrats with more or less autonomy and initiative, this approach brings to our attention the central role that institutions play in structuring political and social life and in processing pressures from political and economic interests, as well as organized groups. "Public vengeance," Barker argues, "depends on certain political institutions and collective agency to give it a legal and political expression" (2009: 12). This view is also articulated by Schoenfeld (2014) in her examination of the delayed emergence of penal modernism in Florida. Intrigued by the failure of penal modernism to take hold in particular regions and states (such as Florida), Schoenfeld found that political arrangements in Florida (specifically a weak state government and power concentrated around local rural White interests), as well as limited state bureaucratic capacity, prevented political and bureaucratic actors from reforming penal institutions. And when reforms did take place — for instance when the state created a parole system in 1941 (decades after most other states) — the legislature consistently under-funded the new programs, thereby undermining their mission:

> "[I]n the first few years of the [Parole] Commission, the legislature appropriated just enough to fund three commissioners and seven district supervisors, who covered anywhere from four to 12 contiguous counties. The lack of state capacity for parole therefore assured that inmates had to wait years before being considered for parole" (2014: 269)

Similarly, few studies provide systematic analyses of the effects of constitutional structure on social policy formation, but Immergut's (1992) research on health insurance in Switzerland, France and Sweden shows that structures do matter. Her findings indicate that political institutions in these three countries decisively shaped the ability of different groups to activate power resources and influence the making of health-insurance policies. Where power is centralized and executive power is insulated from parliamentary and electoral pressures, she argues, there is a greater likelihood that reforms that significantly alter the status quo will be implemented. Where power is dispersed in representative institutions, however, relatively small interest groups are able to block reform legislation. In the same way, Barker's (2009) analysis of the politics of imprisonment in the states of New York, California, and Washington demonstrates that crucial differences in these states' political institutions account for differences in their penal regimes.

But this perspective also challenges the view of the state as a monolithic, impersonal force that defines patterns in politics by taking into account the influence that special interests, political and economic groups, and citizens broadly speaking have on institutions and policy. It is clear that penal actors operate in a context that structures the decisions they make and their ability to influence policy priorities, but as Page's (2012) study of the California Correctional Peace Officers Association (CCPOA) demonstrates, penal actors also mediate how large-scale phenomena translate into penal outcomes and contribute to shaping the field in which they operate. His analysis shows that the successful and powerful labor union that represents correctional employees in California and opposes prisoners' rights and rehabilitation was able to capitalize on the politicization of crime and punishment to push forward an agenda that included toughening prison conditions, hardening sentencing policies, helping to create punitive crime victims' groups, projecting a zero-sum view of the relationship between victims and prisoners (to help victims is to hurt prisoners and vice versa), arguing that California prisoners are "the worst of the worst," and criticizing traditional legal experts (psychologists, criminologists, sociologists, legal scholars, social workers, judges) for lacking "real life" penal expertise. "Because of the union and its counterparts' dominant positions in the penal and related fields, the visions they champion are efficacious" (Page 2012: 162). In the same way Barker (2009) shows that civic engagement — the degree to which ordinary citizens get involved in state politics — influences the nature of the policies created by state political institutions, as well as the extent to which states rely on confinement, by keeping a check on the repressive powers of the state. Together, political structures and practices of civic engagement (i.e., collective agency) form modes of governance upon which better models of carceral state development can be built.

In this chapter, I traced the genealogy of the late modern transformation of criminal punishment in the U.S. and discussed what we have learned from the vast body of theoretical and empirical research regarding the social, political, and cultural processes upon which state penal policies and practices have been built. This literature has identified five broad categories of factors that can be used to build a framework with which to analyze the historically recent expansion of the penal system. As Figure 2.4 indicates, these factors are not distinct from one another — that is, sentencing policies are tied to a certain political rhetoric that seized on crime as a solution to a broader governmental crisis stemming from troublesome social and economic changes. And state-specific modes of governance may mediate the effects of these factors to produce different paths of carceral state development. For the sake of simplicity, however, we can say that they view changes and differences in the scope of penal sanctioning as: (1) an outcome of criminal behavior; (2) a mechanism for the social control of racial minorities and economically marginalized populations; (3) an artifact of electoral politics and ideological conflicts; (4) a product of state governance and practices of civic engagement; and (5) the result of policy choices.

A major limitation of the prison boom literature stems from its myopic focus on incarceration, which constitutes only one penological aspect of the criminal justice system. Studies have concentrated almost exclusively on "front-end sentences" (offenders sent to prison through court sentences), ignoring back-end sentencing (parole revocations) in spite of the fact that it has become a major dynamic of prison intake. This gap in our understanding of the prison boom may stem from the assumption that the factors that explain court sentences are the same as those that affect decisions to revoke a parolee's conditional release. However, as the arguments and evidence set forth in Chapter 3 will show, this statement may overemphasize the similarities between "front-end" and "back-end" sentencing.

Chapter 3

Toward a Conceptual Model of Parole Revocation Rates

Since 1980, the number of parolees revoked and returned to incarceration has grown sevenfold, from 27,000 to about 200,000 (Figure 3.1). This is partly the artifact of a society that has been locking up a staggering number of its citizens over the last 40 years. With the rare exceptions of the people who die in prison, more than 95 percent of inmates are eventually released (Burke 2003), and the vast majority of those (about 80 percent, according to the Bureau of Justice Statistics) are sentenced to a term of supervision upon their release, even when this release was decided by statutes and not by a parole board. As prison populations grow, so does the number of people on supervision; and greater numbers of people on supervision in turn means a larger population at risk of being recommitted for violating parole conditions. Not only has the absolute number of parolees revoked and recommitted increased but, as Figure 3.2 indicates, the relative contribution of parolees to prison admissions has grown as well — from 17 percent of prison admissions nationally in 1980 to about 30 percent in the first decade of the twenty-first century (Glaze and Palla 2005). Since it is doubtful that changes in parolee behavior are behind the increase, this doubling of the contribution of parole revocations to prison admissions suggests that the frequency of *use of revocation as a sanction* has changed.

This is a phenomenon we do not understand very well because scant attention has been paid to a parole system that has been dramatically shifting the landscape of prison admissions. Indeed, the extensive literature devoted to documenting, explaining, and theorizing the changing nature of penal sanctioning in the U.S. has been myopically focused on incarceration: "It is safe to say that parole programs have received less research attention than any other correctional component in recent years" writes Joan Petersilia. "A congressionally mandated evaluation of state and local crime prevention programs included just one parole evaluation among the hundreds of recent studies that were summarized for that effort" (1999:524).

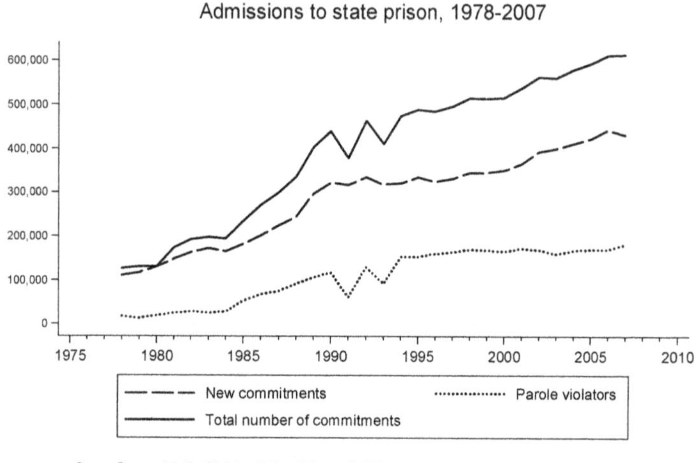

Figure 3.1 Admissions to state prison, 1978-2007

This relative lack of interest extends beyond questions about parole's effectiveness in reducing recidivism and improving reentry outcomes. Parole is a key component of the U.S. criminal justice system, and revocation has become a crucial back-end steering mechanism, yet scholars have neglected to pay sufficient attention to the profound changes in the way that the parole system is managed, how it has responded to the "punitive turn" (i.e., the increasingly punitive criminal justice response to crime that has permeated the culture and the criminal justice system's philosophy of punishment over the last 40 years), and the relationship between parole revocations and the growth of our nation's prison system.

This chapter attempts to unpack the proverbial "black box" of the parole revocation process in order to contextualize the meaning of revocation as a sanction. It also endeavors to identify salient dimensions upon which a conceptual model of the use of revocation can be constructed.

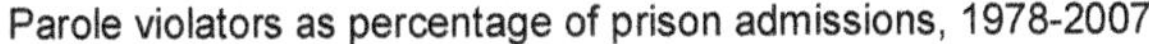

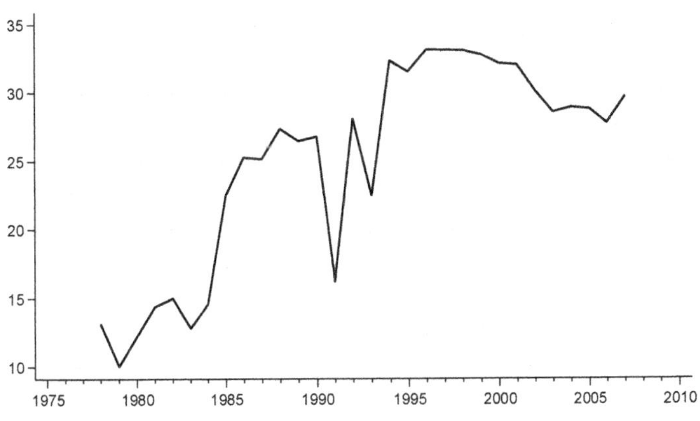

Figure 3.2 Parole violators as percentage of prison admissions, 1978-2007

SOME BACKGROUND

Origins of the modern parole system[12]

The origins of the modern parole system — i.e., a system of early release from prison in exchange for an inmate's promise that he will not commit new crimes and that he will abide by the conditions placed upon his release — can be traced to the seventeenth century conditional pardons and indentures of servitude. However, parole did not become a full-fledged concept until late into the nineteenth century when

---

[12] For more thorough accounts of the development of the modern parole system, see Bottomley (1990); Petersilia (1996); Rothman (1980); or Simon (1993).

widespread transformations in penology started taking place in Western Europe and the United States. The practice did not come to be known as "parole" until its introduction in the United States in the 1870s. Until then, the main goals of punishment were deterrence, retribution, and incapacitation. Accordingly, prisoners were subjected to harsh living and working conditions, as well as brutal physical punishment to ensure obedience. Sentences issued by the courts involved no positive conditioning, and once offenders had served their term they were released into society unconditionally.

Alexander Maconochie (who was in charge of the British penal colony on Norfolk Island, off the coast of Australia, in the mid-1800s) and Sir Walter Crofton (chairman of the Irish Prison Board) are usually credited for developing the concept of the parole system (Petersilia 2003; Ruggles-Brise 1921; Witmer 1927). Crofton's Irish Convict System, for example, was a graduated system aimed at reforming convicts who could earn marks for work, good behavior, and educational improvement; eventually they earned a ticket of leave and their release on parole. While on parole, they were required to report monthly to the police, and they were assigned a special civilian inspector (the ancestor of the modern parole agent) who helped them find work and re-integrate into the community (Petersilia 2003).

In the United States, "good time" laws that permitted a reduction of time served on the basis of good behavior had been on the books since 1817 when New York first enacted such legislation. The goals of these laws were to give prison administrators some control over inmates' behavior, to relieve prison overcrowding, and to help rehabilitate inmates. However, good time legislation alone could not address institutional problems and overcrowding which subsequently developed. In the 1850-60s states (Michigan first among them) began to take steps toward instituting a system of early release by formalizing the powers of the governor to grant conditional pardons (Bottomley 1990). It was not until the 1870s that American penologists followed in the footsteps of European prison reformers and adapted the "Irish system" to the specific needs of the American penal and political context. Michigan penologist Zebulon Brockway, who was appointed superintendent at the newly established Elmira Reformatory for young offenders in New York in 1876, put in place the first American parole system featuring a two-pronged strategy designed to manage prison populations (through indeterminate sentencing) and prepare inmates for release (parole supervision). The concept spread quickly; by 1900 twenty states had introduced parole statutes. This number reached 32 by 1910, 44 by 1922, and by 1930 every U.S. state had adopted both indeterminate sentencing and parole release (Bottomley 1990:322).

Modern parole

Today's parole system strikes an awkward balance between the twin goals of surveillance and service. It is still structured around the same organizing principles of release, supervision and revocation; however, it has also become more closely aligned with the law enforcement community, and the philosophy of punishment upon which parole was based until the 1970s, as well as the way parole operates, have shifted significantly.

The activities and responsibilities of the modern parole system are carried out by two organizational entities — parole boards and departments of corrections — that work either separately (in the case of release and supervision) or together (revocation). Parole release refers to the discretionary authority vested in a governmental entity (some jurisdictions refer to their paroling authority as parole board, others as parole commission, or board of pardons and paroles, etc.) established by law or constitution to release offenders from prison prior to the completion of their sentence. The authority of parole boards was severely challenged starting in the 1970s. Parole boards were criticized for having too much discretion, and their decisions were seen as arbitrary and capricious by some, while others worried that the system was too lenient and offenders were being "let off easy." States moved toward determinate sentencing structures which limited the power of judges and parole boards to set prison terms and transferred this power to legislatures.

While the move to abolish parole boards ended in 1996 (APAI 2005), efforts to impose limits on their authority have continued with the implementation of mandatory minimums, truth-in-sentencing laws, and the exclusion of specific crimes or classes of offenders from consideration for parole (Figure 2.3). As a result, nationally about 18 percent of prison inmates are released mandatorily and unconditionally — that is, under no supervision and without any conditions (Hughes, Wilson, and Beck 2001). The rest, about 4-in-5 prison inmates, are either released discretionarily or released mandatorily with supervision conditions. In other words, many of the boards that have little to no authority over *when* to release inmates continue to have responsibility over the vast majority of offenders for other parole functions such as reviewing release plans, setting parole conditions, approving good time, and handling revocations. Boards also retain full releasing authority over offenders convicted prior to the state's adoption of determinate sentencing (i.e., the abolition of the parole board).

Parole supervision refers to the responsibility vested in a public agency — usually a state department of corrections — for the supervision of offenders during some period of conditional release following incarceration. Just as parole boards came under criticism in the 1970s, so did parole supervision. Support for parole-as-rehabilitation waned, and safety and security became the guiding principles of supervision. Parole officers, whose role used to be to help ensure reentry success by brokering needed services such as job assistance, counseling, and access to chemical dependency programs, have become more surveillance and policing oriented in their outlook. Drug testing, electronic monitoring, and the enforcement of curfews are commonly used, and new technologies make it easier for parole agents to detect violations. Parolees are required to abide by certain conditions; failure to do so can result in revocation of parole. Standard conditions apply to virtually all parolees, and include reporting to the parole agent upon release from prison and meeting with him or her regularly; the frequency of this meeting requirement is determined by the level of supervision. Proper conduct upon release includes not carrying weapons, not committing crimes, seeking and maintaining employment, not leaving the jurisdiction without prior approval from the parole agent, and submitting to searches by police and parole agents. Special conditions are tailored to particular offenders, such as submitting to regular drug testing for substance abusers or staying away from parks, schools, etc. for sex offenders. Parole agents are responsible for ensuring that parolees abide by the conditions of their parole contract. They have the legal authority to carry a weapon, search places, persons and property without a warrant, arrest parolees without probable cause, and confine them without bail – making parole agents "walking court systems" (Petersilia 1999: 482; Simon 1993).

Parole revocation refers to the action that paroling authorities are empowered to take in response to an offender's non-compliance with the conditions of his or her release or for new criminal conduct. The condition violator's conditional release is revoked and s/he is returned to custody for all or part of the remainder of his/her original sentence. Though parolees do have some rights (they must be given written notice of the nature of the violation and the evidence obtained, and they have the right to confront and cross-examine their accusers), the standards of due process are minimal because while under supervision parolees are technically still in the custody of the state.

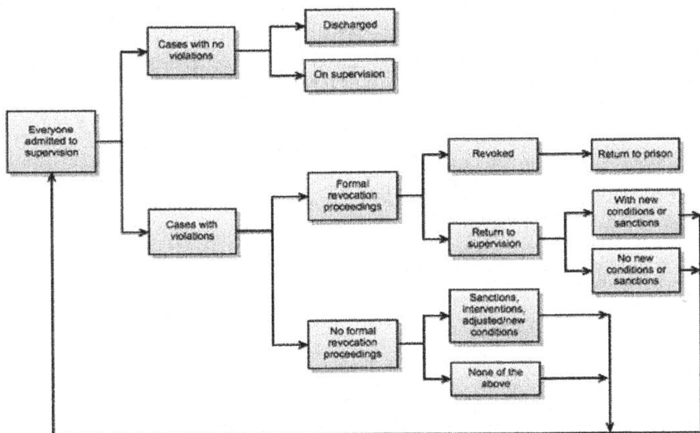

Figure 3.3 Map of the outcomes of parole violations

Figure 3.3 depicts the revocation process. This map oversimplifies the process for the sake of clarity; in reality, the parole revocation process is rather complex. In New Jersey, for instance, the parole revocation process involves 5 supervising parole officers, 14 district supervisors, 26 assistant district supervisors, a large number of senior parole officers, recruits, and the electronic monitoring unit, as well as the prosecutor, police, potential witnesses, counsel for the parolee, and at least two members of the parole board (Burke 2004). The revocation process can take several weeks, and varies considerably from state to state. Typically a violation will come to the attention of the parole agent, who then investigates and determines whether it is a criminal violation (which is usually handled as a new crime and referred to the court system), or a technical violation; in the case of a technical violation, the agent determines whether it is sufficiently severe to warrant revocation or it can be addressed through the use of alternative sanctions in the community. For example, in the case of drug use the agent may require that the parolee attend drug counseling and/or report more frequently to his/her parole agent. If the violation is considered serious, the supervising agency (the parole agent and his supervisor) initiates revocation procedures by reporting violations to the Board, and a warrant is issued for the violator's arrest. The parole board then holds a hearing and makes the final revocation decision. If the board decides to revoke parole parolees are returned to incarceration to serve the remainder of their sentences. What happens between the detection of the violation and the revocation recommendation to the Board varies from state to state, depending on the extent to which supervising agencies are required to use guidelines and risk assessment tools to make decisions about the handling of violations, whether and what range of graduated sanctions they are allowed to use, what violations are subject to mandatory referrals to the Board, how much discretion parole agents have in responding to violations, and whether policy is clearly delineated and communicated.

Invisible punishment

It could be argued that the revocation decision at the "back end" of the criminal justice system is merely the continuing application the original sentence imposed at the "front end" by the courts. The defendants are aware when the sentence is imposed — and it is understood by everyone else involved in the sentencing process — that following their release from prison, they will be subjected to a term of supervision, with conditions, and that failure to abide by those conditions could result in their being re-incarcerated. But Jeremy Travis (2007) argues that parole revocation is a form of punishment and that failure to recognize it as such has allowed the process to remain invisible and to escape the scrutiny of the debates about sentencing (Travis 2002, 2007). The ubiquitous process of adjudicating parole violations should therefore be seen as a sentencing system in its own right, albeit one that shares conceptual and operational similarities with the court sentencing system. In both of these systems, the enforcement agencies of the state (police or parole) are used to detect violations of rules (criminal laws or conditions of supervision), arrest and detain those suspected of those infractions (defendants or parole violators), bring cases and suspects before a neutral adjudicative entity (judge or hearing officer), provide an opportunity for determinations of fact through adversarial process (with some distinctions between the systems), determine guilt (with differing levels of proof) and impose sanctions for violations of those rules, up to and including deprivation of liberty.

Table 3-1 Comparison of front-end and back-end sentencing systems

	Front-end sentencing	Back-end sentencing
Enforcement agency	Police	Parole agency
Accused	Defendant	Parole violator
Adjudicative entity	Court	Parole board, with substantive input of parole agent into sanctioning decision
Appointment of decision-makers	Political	Administrative
Formality	High	Low
Setting	Public	Closed
Procedural protections for accused	Extensive	Few
Evidentiary threshold	High, "beyond a reasonable doubt"	Low(er), "preponderance of the evidence"

These clear parallels notwithstanding, back-end sentencing also departs in important ways from sentencing handled through the court system (see Table 3.1). For one, parole is an administrative agency rather than a political one. Unlike judges and prosecutors, who are elected, parole actors are state employees (parole agents) or they are appointed to their position (parole board). Parole revocation operates somewhat autonomously from the rest of the criminal justice system, according to different rules,[13] with limited exposure to public and

---

[13] The landmark case *Morrissey v. Brewer* (408 U.S. 417, 1972) only established minimum procedural requirements for parole revocations.

judicial scrutiny. Because the standard of evidence used (preponderance of evidence) is more lenient than is required in a court of law (beyond a reasonable doubt), parole revocation is a rather attractive, low-cost alternative to criminal sanctioning, and in some states (such as California) parole boards even handle criminal violation cases that county courts do not successfully prosecute (Grattet, Lin, and Petersilia 2009).

The changing mission of parole

If parole revocation is a form of sentencing, it is important for us to understand its meaning as a sanction. A good place to start is by examining the mission of parole in relation to the changing paradigm of punishment. As Zimring (2001) and many others have pointed out, the growth of imprisonment in the U.S. since the 1970s can be parsed into different eras of expansion, each dominated by a different penological paradigm, a different sanctioning and correctional emphasis. As the mainstream goals of sentencing evolved, so did the mission of parole. This evolution is summarized in Table 3.2.

Rehabilitation. Parole was instituted during the Progressive Era (1870s-1930s), when the long-standing punishment principles of retribution and deterrence were being revisited and penal policy was shaped primarily by the prevailing belief that criminals could be reformed through appropriate individualized treatment. Reformers believed that criminality was not primarily the product of offenders' personal moral failures, but the result of the influence of environmental conditions combined with deficiencies in offenders' attributes and capacities. Crime, therefore, was thought to have easily identifiable and treatable causes. Progressives also believed that the criminal justice system should attempt to rehabilitate as many offenders as possible by tailoring sentences to the specific needs and characteristics of the individual (Rothman 1980; Simon 1993). Judges were to decide prison sentences based on the offender's crime and circumstances, and expressed as a range between the earliest possible time of release (minimum), and the expiration of the sentence (maximum). Prison officials, parole boards, and parole officers were to tailor programs, decide release dates, and create a supervision plan based on the individual's needs and progress toward rehabilitation.

Extensive discretion was the cornerstone of the indeterminate system. However, while rehabilitation may have been the penological ideal of the time, the system struggled to keep its rehabilitative promises and the extensive discretion permitted to key actors came into question by state legislators. Bottomley cautions against romanticizing the rehabilitative intentions behind early parole systems:

"It is doubtful," he explains, "whether [parole] ever really operated consistently ... either in principle or in practice according to the true canons of the rehabilitative model. From that point of view, it was a straw man that never realized the ideals of its more fervent advocates but reacted to the more pressing demands of an ever-increasing prison population and the wider issues of social control" (1990: 326).

Nevertheless, parole did gain legitimacy as the positivist approach to crime and criminals changed penological beliefs about the purpose of punishment, and it became a symbol of the rehabilitative model that shaped punitive practices for most of the twentieth century — so much so, as a matter of fact, that when penal welfarism and the rehabilitative ideal came under attack in the 1970s the parole process bore the major brunt of the criticisms.

Just deserts. In the 1960s and 1970s skepticism about the effectiveness of treatment, combined with criticism of a sentencing decisionmaking model that produced sentences widely seen as arbitrary, capricious, unjustifiably disparate, and racially biased, undermined the credibility of indeterminate and individualized sentencing. States moved away from rehabilitation as the primary purpose of punishment and adopted a "just deserts" approach that emphasized sentencing goals based on greater determinacy, proportionality, and consistency instead. In the process, state legislatures in more than a dozen states eliminated discretionary parole release, and several more severely reduced the authority of their parole boards.

Deterrence and incapacitation. During the 1980s and 1990s, the prevailing law-and-order rhetoric gave rise to calls for harsher crime control measures. The just deserts approach, with its emphasis on equity and proportionality, was abandoned in favor of approaches based principally on incapacitation and deterrence. Tough-on-crime proponents argued that lengthy and mandatory sentences reduced crime by deterring would-be offenders, and states proceeded to adopt a panoply of harsh punishments such as mandatory minimum sentences, three-strikes laws, and truth-in-sentencing. Parole was once again criticized as a symbol of an earlier, "softer" approach to crime. To show their toughness, parole organizations in many states increased the rates at which parole was revoked (see Table 3.1). Rehabilitation efforts, such as they had become, were limited by diminishing resources for prison programming (education, drug and mental health treatment, job training). Moreover, the elimination of discretionary parole release in many states has removed incentives for inmates to participate in programming. Parole practices, then, by increasing time served, decreasing parole releases, and increasing parole revocations, stayed very much in step with the mainstream goals of sentencing and corrections and the larger sentencing paradigm (Tonry 2004).

Table 3-2 Overview of sentencing trends and parole discretion in the U.S., 1920-2007

Sanctioning/correctional emphasis	Time period			
	1920-1970	1970-1980	1980-2000	2000-2007
Rehabilitation	X			
Just deserts		X		
Incapacitation/deterrence			X	
Evidence-based interventions				X
Parole discretion	Extensive	Reduced or eliminated	Some increase but with high structure	Increasing in some states

Source: Burke (2003)

In the last ten years or so, this larger paradigm has begun to show signs of changing once again. Public opinion surveys now indicate that Americans believe that crime prevention is better achieved through rehabilitation than harsh penalties; struggling state economies are forcing political leaders to find ways to curb the unsustainable growth of prisons and corrections budgets; and the rapid growth of the re-entry movement is shifting the focus away from incapacitation and deterrence, and suggesting the need for a new role for parole — one very much reminiscent of parole's origins 150 years ago.

THE MEANING OF REVOCATION AS A SANCTION

Punitiveness: a "thin" concept

The last ten years notwithstanding, it is tempting to take growing incarceration and parole revocation rates as evidence of a "punitive turn" in criminal justice policies that has resulted in increasingly punitive sanctions. But what exactly does punitiveness mean, and how do we know whether penal sanctioning outcomes are a true reflection of this punitiveness? As Matthews (2005), Kutateladze (2009), Hamilton (2014), and others have noted, for all the "ink spilled about the 'punitive obsession'" (Hamilton 2014: 321), punitiveness remains a rather vague, under-theorized or "thin" concept. It is used to characterize individual or public attitudes toward punishment, as well as state crime control policies and practices. Although traditionally associated with retributivist sentiments and policies, Matthews explains, the concept of punitiveness has acquired connotations of irrational "excess": it is "the pursuit of punishment over and above that which is necessary or appropriate [...], a disproportionate use of sanctions and consequently a violation from the principle of proportionality." It is seen as emotionally motivated, "essentially reactive rather than consequentialist" (2005: 178-9).

Commentators have found evidence of these punitive excesses in high imprisonment rates, the use of the death penalty, mandatory sentencing schemes, public shaming sanctions, long prison sentences, prison living conditions, sex offender registry laws, and chain gangs (Borg 1997; Cook 1995; Frost 2008; Garland 2001; Lynch 1993; Neapolitan 2001; Tonry 2001, 2004; Tyler and Boeckmann 1997; Whitman 2003). Yet with the exception of a few scholars (Gordon 1989; Hamilton 2014; Kutateladze 2009; Tonry 2007; Whitman 2003), this complex and multifaceted phenomenon is often reduced to a single dimension that becomes shorthand for a range of other punitive practices. It is widely accepted practice in the criminological literature to use imprisonment rates as a proxy for punitiveness, for example, and to assume that states with high incarceration rates are more punitive than states with low incarceration rates. But as Gordon (1989) found through her factor analysis of 32 indicators of criminal justice policy, states are not uniformly punitive. Rather they make different choices and pursue different penal strategies, therefore incarceration rates are part of a broader penal and political regime that needs to be interpreted as a whole.

The literature is limited in a second, important way. Indeed, the decisions researchers make about how to operationalize the concept of punitiveness may bias their results and their conclusions. Let's take the example of Frost (2008). She focuses on incarceration and argues convincingly that punitiveness has two components: the increasing *propensity* to incarcerate (or revoke parole), and the increase in the duration of incarceration (which she terms *intensity*). Growing prison populations might be the reflection of changes in one or the other dimension, or most likely a combination of the two. Using 2000 data from the National Corrections Reporting Program, Frost constructed measures of propensity and intensity and assigned states a score on each dimension. This allowed her to classify states based on the distribution of scores. Scores greater or less than 1 and -1 indicate that these states are over- or under-punitive compared to other states. Her findings, summarized in Table 3.3, confirm her hypothesis that states ranking high on propensity do not necessarily rank high on intensity. Pennsylvania, for instance, is identified as over punitive on the intensity dimension, but under punitive on the propensity dimension. Frost also found that some states reputed for being very punitive (Alabama, Louisiana, or Mississippi, for example) emerged as only moderately punitive, while Maine, widely considered one of the most lenient states, actually ranks among the most punitive on the "intensity of punishment" dimension.

Frost's approach, while it sheds some light on states' penal philosophies, nevertheless reduces the multi-dimensionality of state punitiveness to two dimensions. In contrast, Kutateladze (2009) sought to take a holistic view of a state's crime control policies and criminal justice activities. He developed a measure of penal harshness based on 44 variables, grouped into five indices: (A) political and symbolic punishment (death penalty, "three strikes" laws); (B) incarceration; (C) the punishment of immorality (prostitution, gambling); (D) conditions of confinement; and (E) juvenile justice. Kutateladze then computed punitiveness scores for each state and each index. Unlike Frost's, his results confirmed the South's reputation for penal harshness: nine out of the ten extremely punitive states in his classification were southern states: Florida, South Carolina, Mississippi, Georgia, Alabama, Texas, Virginia, Maryland, and Delaware. But like Frost he also found that most states are not consistently punitive across all dimensions of his instrument of penal harshness: Maine, for instance, was identified as the least punitive state across four out of five indicators. But on the incarceration index, it ranked as one of the most punitive. Florida emerged as the most punitive state in the country. It is extremely punitive across most dimensions of punitiveness, but ranked very low on the fourth dimension (conditions of confinement). New York appeared minimally punitive for indices A and C, moderately punitive for index B, and more than moderately punitive for indices D and E.

Table 3-3 Classifying states on measures of punitiveness, 2000 (N=34)

		Intensity		
		Under punitive	*Average*	*Over punitive*
	Under punitive	Minnesota	New York Utah	Maine Pennsylvania
Propensity	*Average*	Missouri South Dakota West Virginia	17 states[a]	Florida Maryland Michigan Ohio Texas
	Over punitive	North Dakota	Iowa Nevada	Oklahoma

Source: Frost (2008)

Note: [a] The 17 states are: Alabama, Arkansas, California, Colorado, Georgia, Hawaii, Kentucky, Louisiana, Mississippi, Nebraska, New Hampshire, New Jersey, North Carolina, Oregon, South Carolina, Virginia and Washington.

As Frost's and Kutateladze's analyses demonstrate, our conceptualizations and measures of punitiveness result in different nomenclatures of punitive states and shape our view of the penological topography of the United States. Of course, as Hamilton (2014) recognizes, it is not always practical for researchers to use multi-dimensional criteria of punitiveness in their studies. But by relying on single measures of punitiveness, such as imprisonment rates, we run the risk of grossly misinterpreting the meaning of penal sanctioning outcomes.

The complicated relationship between incarceration and parole revocation

The need for a nuanced and contextualized analysis becomes even more evident when looking at the relationship between parole revocation rates and incarceration rates. Common sense would suggest that if high incarceration rates are indicative of the punitiveness of a jurisdiction, so should high parole revocation rates. Furthermore, the two should go hand in hand—punitive states that incarcerate a large number of people should also be harsh toward their parolees. However, Kutateladze's findings tell us that this may not necessarily be the case and, as it turns out, the overall correlation between incarceration rates and parole revocation rates is very weak (r=.0453). Recent contributions to the literature (discussed in earlier chapters) caution us however against ignoring the substantial and potentially important variations in punishment across locales. Not surprisingly, disaggregating the correlation between incarceration and parole revocation rates by year and by state further complicates the picture. These results are shown below in Figure 3.4 and Figure 3.5.

For most of the 1978-2007 period, the coefficients tend to be very modest (hovering around and under .2) and negative. Only sporadically in the 1980s is the relationship between incarceration rates and parole revocation rates ever positive. Even then, it remains small. Therefore it appears that it would be a mistake to look at parole revocation rates (or incarceration rates, for that matter) as telling us something about how punitive a state is. As Hamilton points out, "the use of punitiveness as an umbrella term for policies and practices which criminologists simply consider undesirable while ignoring other more inconvenient truths is not sustainable, nor desirable" (2014: 338). This point is further illustrated by Figure 3.5, which shows that in some of the states reputed for being the most punitive, the relationship between incarceration and parole revocation rates is negative (this is the case for Mississippi and South Carolina, for example), or close to zero (Alabama, Texas). Perhaps even more importantly, Figure 3.5 shows a great deal of sub-national variation.

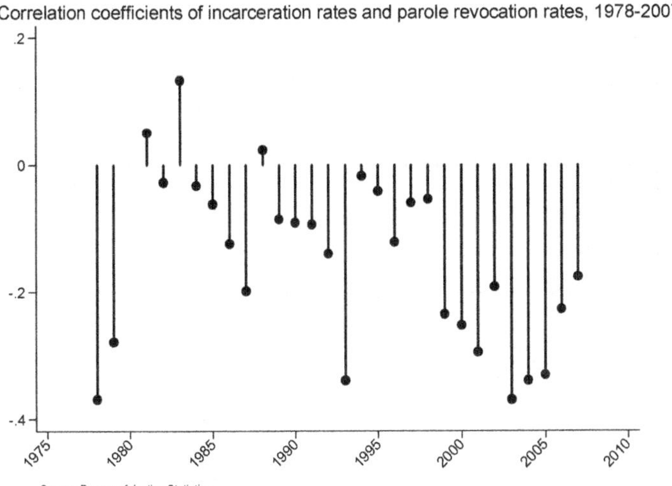

Figure 3.4 Correlation coefficients of incarceration rates and parole revocation rates, 1978-2007

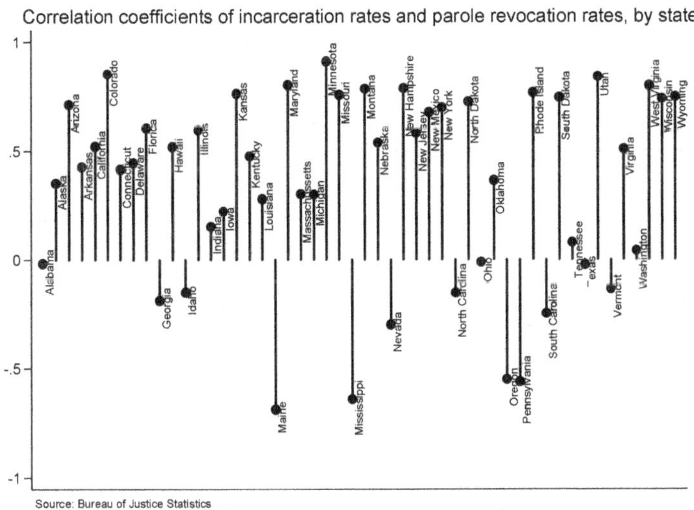

Figure 3.5 Correlation coefficients of incarceration rates and parole revocation rates, by state, 1978-2007

The inconvenient truth, as Jeremy Travis noted, is that changes in parole revocation rates may not be a reflection of the influence of punitive policies as much as a sign that parole is adapting to practical constraints (prison overcrowding, for instance) or to the lack of viable alternative sanctions in the community. It is also possible that more stringent parole management practices have more to do with "the pursuit of performance indicators and a more rigid commitment to the achievement of designated targets and objectives" than with the assessment of risk or any punitive sentiments translated into harsh policies (Matthews 2005: 187).

BUILDING A CONCEPTUAL MODEL OF PAROLE REVOCATION

Factors affecting rates of parole revocation

Whether parolees successfully complete the term of their supervision is generally understood to be a function of three main factors: characteristics of the individual, community environment in which they reside, and the administration of parole (Grattet et al. 2009). Individual-level characteristics — which include static factors (race, gender, age, criminal history) and dynamic factors (substance abuse, mental health issues, etc.) — have been a primary focus of the research on recidivism and parole violations, and their effects are by now relatively well documented (for a review of this extensive literature, see Harcourt 2007).

While individual characteristics do have an important influence on criminal behavior, recidivism and violations of parole, criminologists as far back as the 1940s have hypothesized that neighborhood dynamics mediate this relationship. Social disorganization theorists, for example, have long emphasized the role of poverty, ethnic heterogeneity, and residential turnover, arguing that these elements increase the attractiveness of crime and undermine informal social control in a neighborhood (Bursik and Grasmick 1993; Sampson, Raudenbush, and Earls 1997; Shaw and McKay 1942). Moreover, a recent study (Kubrin and Stewart 2006) of recidivism among parolees found economic disadvantage to be correlated with the risk of parolee recidivism (Kubrin and Stewart 2006), which dovetails with studies showing that communities plagued by crime, poverty, and unemployment lack the resources and social support necessary to help ex-offenders transition back into society successfully (Fagan, West, and Holland 2003; Gephart 1997; Harding 2003; Morenoff, Sampson, and Raudenbush 2001; Sampson, Morenoff, and Gannon-Rowley 2002; Sampson, Morenoff, and Raudenbush 2005).

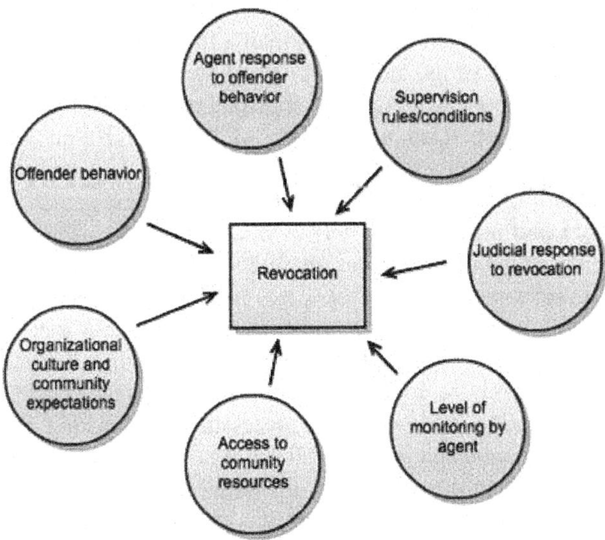

Figure 3.6 Factors that can impact rates of parole revocation

As helpful as the theoretical and empirical scholarship on individual characteristics and neighborhood contexts is in understanding criminal (re)offending, it sheds little light on the institutional factors — i.e., variation in the way the criminal justice system responds to parole violations or behavior that could potentially lead to violations. Ironically, these are perhaps the most proximate determinants of spatial, and maybe temporal, variation in rates of parole revocation. The forces driving revocations are complex and difficult to assess. As shown in Figure 3.6 revocations stem from a combination of the failure of the offender to comply with some condition of parole, along with the combined actions of a parole supervision agency and of a paroling authority. The revocation process involves multiple stakeholders, with a complex set of procedural requirements, and with typically very little policy guidance or oversight. Not surprisingly, this set of circumstances can result in significant variation in the rate of revocation. A 1995 study commissioned by the North Carolina legislature to investigate parole revocation processes in the state illustrates this point. The study found that the types of violations that resulted in revocation varied between the counties observed, and also between officers within the same agency. They also found that the programming available to parolees varied widely between counties. Finally, they found that responses to initial violations varied among parole officers, with some relying on a variety of treatment programs and others immediately filing for revocation (North Carolina Division of Adult Probation and Parole Revocation Task Force 1995).

According to a National Institute of Corrections study of parole violations and prison admissions in Georgia, Kansas, New Jersey and Rhode Island, parole violations are quite common; 71-84 percent of all cases under supervision had at least one violation noted in their file (Burke 2004). The fact that revocation rates in the four states included in the study ranged from 20 to 60 percent suggests that the states do not respond uniformly to conditions of release violations. Understanding parole revocation rates therefore necessitates unpacking the social, political, economic and institutional processes that underlie state parole policies and practices; this is work that scholars have yet to undertake.

This gap in the literature leaves one with little direction. Insofar as parole is an intrinsic part of the criminal justice system, one can assume that, to a great extent, parole policies and practices are subjected to the same macro-level processes that have shaped and transformed the system as a whole. As Garland (2001a) and others (Allen 1981) have described, we have seen in the last four decades a reversal of the assumptions that shaped crime control and punishment for the better part of the 20th century — *including* parole. Perhaps even more than other elements of the criminal justice system, all aspects of parole (release, supervision, and revocation) came under criticism in the 1960s and 70s, and the decades that followed saw the nature and application of parole toughen from supervision and the provision of services to enhanced surveillance and more frequent punishment through recommitment — a reflection of the widespread transformations of crime control in the U.S. However, the proposition that front-end and back-end sentencing have been affected by, and have responded to, these changes in similar ways has yet to be rigorously tested. This discussion also demonstrates that organizational factors are likely to play a greater role in parole revocation rates than they do for incarceration rates.

Limitations of analyses of parole revocation rates

There is a major obstacle (and perhaps one of the reasons parole has been neglected in the literature) that researchers come across when trying to study the determinants of parole revocation — namely, the lack of available aggregate data. States themselves often collect only the most rudimentary data in this area. As part of the National Corrections Reporting Program (NCRP) run by the Bureau of Justice Statistics, states are asked to report aggregate data on their prison populations, as well as parole, but not all states contribute their data, and the NCRP has notoriously poor, unreliable data in the area of parole revocations. As a result, quantitative studies are missing salient dimensions of revocation rates. It is difficult to assess the influence of caseloads[14] on parole revocation rates for example, because data on parole agents are difficult to locate. Short of contacting each state (or perhaps even each country) individually, researchers have no way of knowing how many parole agents are employed by each state's supervising agency. This is an important limitation that future research will need to overcome.

---

[14] According to the focal concerns perspective, criminal justice decision makers operate with "bounded rationality" (Jones 1999; March and Simon 1958; Simon 1991), meaning that they "seek to minimize the costs and maximize the benefits of their decisions" but they do so "with imperfect or limited information, and are further constrained by limited time, resources, and cognitive capacities" (Lin et al. 2012). Decision-makers therefore rely on "cues" or attributions in order to make sanctioning decisions (Albonetti 1991; Carroll 1978; Shaver 1975): the offender's perceived threat to public safety, or practical constraints of the institutional bureaucracy such as court caseload pressures or prison overcrowding, for instance (Lin, Grattet, and Petersilia 2012, 2010; Johnson, Ulmer, and Kramer 2008; Huebner and Bynum 2006, 2008; Ulmer, Bader, and Gault 2008; Julmer and Johnson 2004).

Chapter 4

Studying Penal Sanctioning

In this chapter I describe the data collection techniques, the operationalization and measurement of the variables, and the analytic strategy used in this book to investigate the state-level determinants of incarceration rates and parole revocation rates in the United States between 1978 and 2007.

DATA COLLECTION

Prior research provided an initial reference point for the types of factors or general areas likely to have an impact on incarceration rates and parole revocation rates. As outlined in Chapter 2, these factors broke down into the six general categories — crime rates, symbolic threats, political culture, state governance, sentencing structure, and demographic controls. These categories are used to develop a conceptual framework and construct the dataset used in this analysis.

Three types of sources were relied upon to collect the data required. The majority of the data were obtained from published and unpublished reports issued by state government or federal agencies such as the U.S. Census Bureau or the Bureau of Justice Statistics. The data on crime, symbolic threats, practical constraints and demographic controls were all obtained from such official sources. For the most part, the most recent data were available in electronic form that could be downloaded directly into Excel spreadsheets. However, some reports covering the early years in the study were only available in hard copy; these data had to be located in library archives (or purchased from government agencies) and entered into Excel manually.

The analyses reported here also use validated scales or indices created by other researchers. This is the case for the measures of citizen ideology (Berry, Ringquist, Fording and Hanson 1998), gubernatorial power (Beyle 2004), voter turnout (United States Elections Project 2010), and social capital (Putnam 2000). These sources are described more fully in the next section. These data and all associated documentation are publicly available and can be downloaded from their creators' websites.

Data on states' sentencing structures were the most difficult to locate and the most time-consuming to compile; the states offer a complex patchwork of criminal justice policies that has not been rigorously or comprehensively documented by any one agency or professional organization. Organizations such as the American Probation and Parole Association or the Association of Paroling Authorities International provided some information, but finding complete and accurate data often involved researching the history of sentencing policies for each state and cross-checking the information against other published sources.

Periodization

Broadly speaking, the trajectory of penological transformation that took place in the United States after the punitive turn is one that is marked by increasing incarceration and parole revocation rates, in the context of increasing crime rates, a hardening of political discourse and increasing constraints being imposed upon sentencing decisions, both at the front end (courts) and at the back end (parole revocation) of the criminal justice system. However, as demonstrated in Chapter 2, it is likely that the influence of the various factors at play was not felt equally throughout the period under study. Crime rates, for instance, increased dramatically through the 1980s, then declined just as dramatically from the 1990s on. In order to tease out the influence of these factors, capture historically contingent phenomena, and explain the variation in contemporary state penological regimes, the analytical strategy includes periodized analyses.

Undoubtedly periodization produces historical narratives with a neat (sometimes convenient), but somewhat subjective and artificial sense of coherence and rupture that rarely existed so clearly in reality. Nevertheless it has long been used in historical and sociological analysis to simplify history, identify turning points (dates or events), or demarcate periods and their unique underlying logics and social outcomes (Campbell and Schoenfeld 2013; Haydu 1998; Hernes 1976; Isaac and Griffin 1989; Katznelson 1997). Various strategies can be used to divide the post-Civil Rights era into analytical periods for the purpose of investigating the prison boom. For instance, based on the empirical literature on mass imprisonment that focuses on ideology and political culture, one could use political trends (Goldwater-Nixon Southern strategy; Reagan-G.H.W. Bush era; the co-optation of the law-and-order message by Clinton) as cut points. Rather than focus on ideology and political developments however, I chose to divide the study into three time periods (1978-1988; 1989-1998; 1999-2007) on the basis of three phases in the growth of incarceration rates at the turn of the twenty-first century. Doing so will hopefully allow me to identify and distinguish the factors responsible for the early build-up of incarceration, those that sustained its growth, and finally those that explain the recent decarceration trend.

DATA

Operationalization and measurement of variables

Table 4.1 gives a summary of all variables used in the empirical chapters (information about data sources can be found in Appendix A). The variables are organized according to the concepts they measure. Descriptive statistics for the entire dataset, as well as descriptive statistics stratified by time period (1978-88; 1989-98; 1999-2007), are provided in Tables 4.2-4.5.

Table 4-1 Description of variables

Concepts	Measures	Type/Unit	Years
	State prisoners	Count	1978-2007
	Parolees revoked	Count	1978-79, 1981-2007
Crime			
	Violent crime	Rate	1978-2007
	Property crime	Rate	1978-2007

Table 4-1 Description of variables (Cond't)

Concepts	Measures	Type/Unit	Years
Symbolic threats			
	% African-American	Rate	1978-2007
	% Hispanic	Rate	1981-2007
	% employed	Rate	1978-2007
	% below poverty	Rate	1980-2007
	Personal income per capita	2007 dollars	1978-2007
Political culture			
	Governor's party	Categorical	1978-2007
	Citizen ideology	Index	1978-2007
State governance			
	Gubernatorial power	Index	1978-2007
	State social capital	Index	1978-2007
	Voter turnout	Rate	1980-2008
Practical constraints			
	Corrections expenditures per capita	2007 dollars	1978-2007
Sentencing structure			
	Structured sentencing	Categorical	1978-2007
	Sentencing guidelines	Categorical	1978-2007
	Parole board authority	Categorical	1978-2007
	Determinate sentencing	Dichotomous	1978-2007
Demographic controls			
	% population aged 18-24	Rate	1978-2007
	% metropolitan population	Rate	1978-80, 1983-88, 1990-2007
	Marriage rate	Rate	1978-80, 1985, 1987-98, 2000-07
	State population	Count	1978-2007

Table 4-2 Descriptive statistics

Variable	N	Mean	SD	Min	Max
Prison population	1500	16816.72	25093.74	186	175512
Incarceration rate	1500	294.71	170.27	28.48	926.69
Parole population	1489	9831.63	19664.6	28	123764
Total # of revocations	1345	2422.63	8009.31	0	81431
Crime index	1500	2.20e-10	1	-1.96	3.50
Economic threat index	1500	-1.04991	1	-3.31	2.26
% Black	1500	9.75	9.32	.22	37.34
% Hispanic	1500	6.26	8.22	.02	44.35
Citizen ideology	1500	48.16	15.45	8.44	95.97
Party of governor	1500	.50	.53	0	2
Civic engagement	1498	2.82e-10	1	-4.01	2.80
Gubernatorial power	1500	3.57	.56	1.8	5
Corrections index	1500	5.83e-10	1	-1.98	3.86
Discretionary release	1500	.25	.44	0	1
Voluntary guidelines	1500	.28	.45	0	1
Presumptive guidelines	1500	.10	.31	0	1
State population	1500	5164239	5628873	401851	3.66e+07
Marriage rate	1500	10.96	12.96	4.52	159.29
Metropolitan population	1500	66.91	21.06	11.57	102.34
% 18-24-yr olds	1500	10.90	1.53	7.95	15.66

                    Penal Sanctioning in the United States

Table 4-3 Descriptive statistics, 1978-1988

Variable	N	Mean	SD	Min	Max
Prison population	550	8094.57	9716.68	186	76171
Incarceration rate	550	167.35	85.99	28.49	493.65
Parole population	543	5019.35	8552.41	93	77827
Total # of revocations	465	913.61	2986.37	0	42851
Crime index	550	.13	1.01	-1.83	3.32
Economic threat index	550	-.50	.95	-3.06	2.27
% Black	550	9.30	9.12	.22	35.40
% Hispanic	550	4.43	6.84	.02	37.95
Citizen ideology	550	46.09	16.31	9.75	93.91
Party of governor	550	.38	.49	0	2
Civic engagement	548	-.01	1.03	-4.01	2.80
Gubernatorial power	550	3.76	.69	1.8	5
Corrections index	550	-.71	.68	-1.98	1.74
Discretionary release	550	.18	.38	0	1
Voluntary guidelines	550	.2	.40	0	1
Presumptive guidelines	550	.04	.19	0	1
State population	550	4657762	4901615	401851	2.85e+07
Marriage rate	550	12.58	16.54	6.74	159.29
Metropolitan population	550	62.99	22.23	11.57	102.34
% 18-24-yr olds	550	12.47	1.08	9.36	15.66

Table 4-4 Descriptive statistics, 1989-1998

Variable	N	Mean	SD	Min	Max
Prison population	500	18123.03	24540.33	451.00	160127
Incarceration rate	500	317.10	141.14	69.78	746.98
Parole population	498	11701.92	22118.67	33.00	121141
Total # of revocations	485	2698.80	7705.07	0.00	70135
Crime index	500	0.27	1.05	-1.77	3.50
Economic threat index	500	-1.14	0.88	-3.32	1.49
% Black	500	9.80	9.41	0.26	37.22
% Hispanic	500	6.17	8.12	0.43	42.62
Citizen ideology	500	48.11	13.89	9.25	89.57
Party of governor	500	0.55	0.56	0.00	2.00
Civic engagement	500	0.01	1.01	-2.40	2.48
Gubernatorial power	500	3.46	0.44	2.30	4.70
Corrections index	500	0.21	0.91	-1.76	3.24
Discretionary release	500	0.26	0.44	0	1
Voluntary guidelines	500	0.31	0.46	0	1
Presumptive guidelines	500	0.13	0.34	0	1
State population	500	5163906	5631734	453401	32700000
Marriage rate	500	10.84	11.76	5.43	103.92
Metropolitan population	500	67.27	20.89	25.83	100.00
% 18-24-yr olds	500	10.00	0.83	7.95	13.65

Table 4-5 Descriptive statistics, 1999-2007

Variable	N	Mean	SD	Min	Max
Prison population	450	26025.67	33726.01	943	175512
Incarceration rate	450	425.50	167.45	124.99	926.69
Parole population	448	13585.34	24666.96	28	123764
Total # of revocations	395	3859.97	11425.34	0	81431
Crime index	450	-0.46	0.74	-1.96	1.50
Economic threat index	450	-1.623	0.81	-3.24	0.55
% Black	450	10.26	9.46	0.33	37.34
% Hispanic	450	8.60	9.25	0.57	44.35
Citizen ideology	450	50.76	15.66	8.45	95.97
Party of governor	450	0.59	0.53	0	2
Civic engagement	450	0.002	0.96	-2.08	2.49
Gubernatorial power	450	3.47	0.43	2.7	4.3
Corrections index	450	0.63	0.88	-1.26	3.87
Discretionary release	450	0.34	0.47	0	1
Voluntary guidelines	450	0.34	0.47	0	1
Presumptive guidelines	450	0.16	0.37	0	1
State population	450	5783635	6360411	479602	3.66E+07
Marriage rate	450	9.11	8.12	4.51	71.49
Metropolitan population	450	71.30	18.79	27.70	99.99
% 18-24-yr olds	450	9.97	0.90	7.95	14.14

Dependent variables

The dependent variables in the analyses are the incarceration rate (Chapter 5), and the parole revocation rate (Chapter 6). In both cases data were obtained from the Bureau of Justice Statistics (BJS).

The main source of data on prisoner counts is the BJS's *National Prisoner Statistics* series (NPS), which has been collecting statistics on prisoners since 1926. NPS reports provide annual and semiannual national and state-level data on the number of prisoners in state and federal prison facilities, as well as aggregate inmate demographics (age, race, and sex); inmates held in private facilities and local jails; system capacity; noncitizens; and persons under age 18. The BJS collects data from the 50 state departments of corrections and from the District of Columbia. In Chapter 5, the analyses use the raw counts as the dependent variable. When analyzing parole revocation rates in Chapter 6, incarceration *rates* — the number of prisoners under state or federal jurisdiction sentenced to more than one year, per 100,000 state residents — is used as an independent variable (this variable is one of the items in the *corrections index*).

Because there is no single consistent source of data for parole revocations, state parole revocation data were drawn from various data collections published by BJS: the *Correctional Populations* series, *Prisoners* series, and *Probation and Parole in the US* series. These reports provide information on the number of adults on state and federal parole at the beginning and end of each year, the number of adults entering and exiting (including type of exit: completion of supervision; revocation for a technical violation; or return to incarceration with a new sentence) parole supervision during the year, and the characteristics of adults under the supervision of parole agencies. For the period 1999-2005, BJS provided unpublished data from the *Annual Parole Survey* series. No parole revocation data were available for 1980.

Independent variables

Crime. Property and index crime[15] figures from the FBI's Uniform Crime Reports (UCR), available from BJS, are used for the crime variable. The UCR is a voluntary law enforcement program that

---

[15] Index crime includes rates of reported murder, rape, robbery, aggravated assault, burglary, larceny, and auto theft.

provides a nationwide view of crime based on the submission of statistics by law enforcement agencies throughout the country. Crime rates represent the numbers of property and violent crimes per 100,000 resident population. These data are known to be imperfect; their reliability is limited by the extent to which reported crime rates reflect local policing practices that target certain crimes or neighborhoods, variations in how police agencies count crimes, and victim reporting behaviors. In addition, because not all local law enforcement agencies provide data for complete reporting periods, the FBI uses estimation techniques to impute missing data. Nonetheless, the UCR crime statistics are the most common source of crime data and the most likely to be used by lawmakers when making decisions about criminal justice policies. Based on the results of a principal components factor analysis, property and violent crime rates were combined into a single *crime* index; the resulting index based on factor scores is used in the analyses.

<u>Symbolic threats</u>. Consistent with past research (Britt 2000; Kautt 2002; Ulmer and Johnson 2004), and as advocated by Kane (2003), the contextual effects of racial and ethnic threat are examined separately. They are measured by the *percentage* of a state's population that is *Black* and *Hispanic*, respectively. The U.S. Census Bureau provided data on state Black populations for 1978-1990. Since the Census Bureau did not collect data on Hispanic populations pre-1980, only 1981-2007 data are included in the analysis. For the remainder of the period (1990-2007) both Black and Hispanic population data were obtained from the Centers for Disease Control bridged-race population estimates. To account for the possible non-linear effects of racial composition (Bridges and Crutchfield 1988; Kane 2003; Hawkins and Hardy 1989; Oliver and Yocom 2004; Yates 1997; Yates and Fording 2005), percentage Black was transformed into a variable coded "0" = "0-2% Black," "1" = "2-15% Black," and "2" = "Over 15% Black," and entered into the analysis as a set of dummy variables.

The contextual effects of economically marginalized populations are assessed using three different measures. The first, percent employed, refers to the annual average of the percentage of civilian non-institutionalized population 16 years and over that is employed. Unemployment figures only take into account people who are actively looking for a job and they do not include discouraged workers who have stopped looking for work. This means that the unemployment rate underestimates unemployment and presents an overly optimistic view of economic conditions. Consequently I chose to use the <u>employment rate</u> in my analyses. Annual employment data were drawn from the Bureau of Labor Statistics.

The U.S. Census Bureau's *Current Population Survey* provided data for the second measure of economic marginalization: poverty rate. The poverty rate is the percentage of the resident population below the established poverty level. The third measure relating to economic well-being is personal income per capita, a variable that measures the relative wealth of a state. These data were obtained from the U.S. Census Bureau *Annual Survey of State Government Finances and Census of Governments*. All values were adjusted to 2007 constant dollars using the Consumer-Production Index and are expressed per capita.

<u>Political culture</u>. Republican control of the executive branch is captured with a variable coded "0" = "Democrat," "1" = "Republican," and "2" if the governorship switched parties mid-year, or the governor was an Independent. These data were compiled by Carl Klarner[16] from the *Book of the States* publications. They are entered into the analysis as a set of dummy variables (the reference category is Democrat).

To investigate the influence of the ideological preferences of the state's residents, the models include a validated (Brace et al. 2004; Schneider & Jacoby 2006) measure of *citizen political ideology* originally developed by Berry, Ringquist, Fording and Hanson (1998). After estimating the ideology of citizens in each congressional district by inferring public opinion based on interest group ratings of elected representatives, Berry and colleagues average scores across districts to yield a state-level measure of citizen ideology (on a scale of 0-100, "0" being the most conservative, and "100" being the most liberal) for every year since 1975. This method for estimating citizen ideology rests on the assumption that there is a strong correspondence between the ideological preferences of voters and elected officials. Though the correlation should be positive, the correspondence is not perfect because people vote for candidates for reasons beyond ideology, including partisanship, incumbency, and policy positions (Cohen 2006). While imperfect, this measure of citizen ideology[17] is superior to

---

[16] http://www.indstate.edu/polisci/klarnerpolitics.htm (accessed June 2014).

[17] Citizen ideology data updated through 2008 were downloaded from http://www.uky.edu/~rford/stateideology.html (accessed June 2014).

data from national surveys because national surveys use a sampling design aimed to accurately describe the nation, not individual states. As a result, state-level estimates of citizen ideology may be imprecise or biased (Brace et al. 2002).

State governance. Consistent with arguments presented by Barker (2003, 2006) and others, *gubernatorial power* is used as an indicator of the degree of centralization of political authority in the state: the stronger the governors' powers, the more centralized the political authority. The Index of Governors' Institutional Powers (Beyle 2004[18]) is a 5-point scale that measures the degree to which governors control budgets, legislation, appointments, political parties, the strength of veto power, and the length of tenure, including the presence or absence of term limits. Beyle computed scores for each state starting in 1960. *Civic engagement* is measured with two variables: voter turnout rate, and the state's social capital score. Data for voter turnout rates are drawn from the United States Election Project.[19] This measure of voter turnout is based on the vote for highest office divided by the voting-eligible population (VEP). The VEP is constructed by adjusting the voting-age population (VAP) for non-citizens and ineligible felons, based on state law. Because of the difficulty in finding pre-1980 data on disenfranchised felons and on citizen voting-age population estimates, the United States Election Project does not provide voter turnout rates prior to 1980. I also rely on Putnam's (2000) computations of state social capital scores. Putnam used two sources of data, the *General Social Surveys* and the *DDB Needham Life Style Surveys* to create a measure of social capital based on civic participation: how often people attend local town meetings, participate in local and state politics, how much people trust one another, etc. Voter turnout rate and social capital were combined into a *civic engagement* index, where higher values indicate higher levels of civic participation.

Sentencing structure. As explained in Chapter 2, policies may influence sentencing by constraining judicial discretion through the implementation of structured sentencing, and/or shifting the locus of discretion by eliminating or limiting parole boards' authority (see

---

[18] http://www.unc.edu/~beyle/gubnewpwr.html (accessed June 2014).

[19] http://elections.gmu.edu/voter_turnout.htm (accessed June 2014)

Figure 2.3); the former controls sentencing decisions and the length of the prison terms imposed at the front-end, while the latter controls releases and time served at the back-end (Stemen 2005). Data on states' sentencing structures were compiled from multiple official and secondary sources.

At the front-end, states sought to create more "structure" in their system through two similar but distinct mechanisms. The first, presumptive sentencing, requires judges to impose the sentences based solely on the severity of offenses and sanctions recommended by statutes. The second, sentencing guidelines, are procedures guiding sentencing decisions based on the severity of the offense committed as well as the criminal history of the offender. Guidelines can be presumptive (judges are required to impose the recommended sentence), or voluntary (judges are not required to impose the recommended sentence). The variable *presumptive sentencing* is a dummy variable coded "1" to denote the presence of presumptive sentencing in a state. Two dummy variables, *voluntary guidelines* and *presumptive guidelines*, indicate whether states use voluntary or presumptive guidelines.

Parole board authority is used as a proximate measure of discretion at the back-end of the system. Even in states where parole has not been abolished, the authority of the parole board varies widely. A number of parole boards still enjoy full authority, while others have seen their powers greatly limited by statutes. The Association of Paroling Authorities International (APAI) has been surveying releasing authorities in all 50 states annually since 1997. The surveys collect data on a variety of topics, ranging from the structure of the releasing authority, the general sentencing framework within which the releasing authority operates, parole release decision-making processes, conditions of supervision, and supervision levels to the paroling authority's role (if any) with offenders who were supervised in the community, paroling authority's role and process (if any) in responding to violations of community supervision and revoking conditional release. APAI's survey data (1997-2007) were used to create the variable *parole board authority*, coded according to APAI's classification scheme: "0" if the state parole board has no authority, "1" if its authority is limited, "2" if the board enjoys full authority. Since APAI started its surveys in 1997, no information was produced for the period between 1978 and 1996. Filling this gap involved researching the recent history of each state's paroling authority, locating relevant policies and their changes, and consulting secondary sources (reports by state-level professional organizations, for example). The information gathered was then used to calculate parole board authority scores for the period 1978-1996. This measure appears in the analyses as a series of dummy variables with "no parole board authority" as the reference category.

Control variables

The analyses include three control variables.[20] In keeping with the argument that the decrease in informal social control associated with breakdowns in the family, or larger relative numbers of non-intact families, may be accompanied by a greater reliance on formal social control (such as corrections), this study includes a *marriage rate* variable. Marriage rate is the number of marriages per 1,000 persons. Data on marriages were collected from the Statistical Abstracts.

Similarly, one might expect that larger urban states devote more resources to formal social control because informal social control decreases with larger populations (Wirth 1938; Land, McCall, and Cohen 1990). Based on this premise, the models include a measure of *metropolitan population* defined as the percentage of the state's population living in areas categorized by the U.S. Census Bureau as metropolitan statistical areas (MSAs).

---

[20] Citing the fact that there is a high incidence of mental illness among inmates, and that the mentally ill are more likely to commit crimes, some scholars have argued that the de-institutionalization of the mentally ill (which started in the 1960s), may be partly responsible for the increases in incarceration rates (Harcourt 2006; Palermo, Smith and Liska 1991). However there are several reasons to believe that these claims exaggerate the role of de-institutionalization in the prison boom. Demographic differences between inmates and mental patients are one reason: inmates tend to be young, male, and minority. By contrast, mental patients tend to be older and female. In addition, some studies (Raphael 2008) suggest that deinstitutionalization accounts for no more than five percent of the increases in incarceration in recent decades. Consequently, this demographic factor is not included in the analyses reported here.

Finally, the models control for the percentage of the population that is between the ages of 18 and 24 because those in their late teens and early twenties are most prone to criminal behavior. Data were obtained from the U.S. Census Bureau.

Data reduction techniques

The dataset contains a large number of variables, some of which are highly correlated. Principal components factor analysis was employed to explore the underlying structure of the data. Examination of the rotated solutions yielded four stable and interpretable factors based on the eigenvalue-one (or Kaiser criterion) and interpretability. The items in each scale were averaged, then standardized for generating the resulting index. In the case of the economic threat index, the scale is reverse-coded so that higher scores would indicate higher levels of economic threat. Table 4.6 indicates which items were used in the scales and provides each scale's alpha coefficient.

Missing data for poverty rate were imputed prior to averaging the items into the scale.

Missing data and imputation

Whenever possible, data were collected for all states (N=50) and all years (T=30) in the study. However, some data were not available for a few variables in a few state-years. This was the case for marriage rates (missing 1981-84, 1986, and 1999); metropolitan population (missing 1981-82 and 1989); and poverty rate (missing 1978-79). Linear interpolation was used to estimate the missing data with the Stata command "ipolate" (for example: by id: ipolate var year, gen(newvar)). Using interpolated data is not an important limitation here because the amount of missing data is rather small, and marriage rates, urbanization, and poverty rates generally follow stable, uniform growth patterns.

Missing parole revocation data were not imputed because doing so would be methodologically problematic and conceptually unsound. Consequently, 204 state-years were lost to missing data in the analyses of parole revocation rates. Pooled time-series estimators, however, are considered robust to limited disparate missing value patterns (Johnson and DiNardo 1997; Woolridge 2002).

Table 4-6 Summary of scales

Scales	Measures	Cronbach's alpha
Crime	Violent crime rate Property crime rate	.7458
Economic threat	% employed Poverty rate Personal income per capita	.8157
Civic engagement	Voter turnout rate State social capital score	.8608
Corrections	Corrections spending Incarceration rate	.7652

SPECIFICATION AND ESTIMATION

Pooled time series cross-sectional design

To assess the influence of the factors described above on incarceration rates and parole revocation rates a multiple time series or pooled time series cross-sectional (TSCS) design is used that combines data from all 50 states over 30 years (1978-2007). TSCS designs offer several advantages over time both series and cross-sectional approaches. For one, the limited number of spatial units or of available data over time sometimes means that time series and cross sectional designs suffer from an imbalance between too many explanatory variables and too few cases, in which case the number of explanatory variables exceeds the degrees of freedom required to model the relationship between dependent and independent variables; this is a violation of a basic assumption of standard statistical analysis. TSCS analysis increases the ratio of cases to variables by pooling the data (each state-year is a case), thereby increasing the power of statistical analyses and allowing for more fully specified models (Schmidt 1997). Second, pooled models permit the investigation of the effects of variables whose variability is negligible or non-existent across time or space (Hicks 1994; Podesta 2002). Third, pooled models capture not only temporal or spatial variation, but variation across these two dimensions simultaneously, allowing researchers to examine trends over time within individual states as well as the impact of nation-wide phenomena on all states. Finally, by using each state as a control for the other states, the pooled TSCS model controls for missing variables that may cause observed differences between states.

Fixed- vs. random-effects models

Pooled data are typically analyzed using fixed-effects or random-effects models (Hsiao 1986; Mundlak 1978; Pindyck and Rubinfeld 1991), either of which can be applied to test the theoretically based hypotheses that state incarceration and state parole revocation numbers are driven by crime rates, symbolic threats, state political conditions, practical constraints, and criminal justice policies. The key differences between the two models are based on the assumptions made by each about the form of the covariance matrix, and the treatment given to omitted variables.

The fixed-effects estimator, sometimes called "within" estimator because it uses variation *within* a state and disregards variation *between* states, examines differences in intercepts, assuming the same slopes and constant variance across states. It does so by including a dummy for each state, which allows each state to have a different intercept and guards against omitted variable bias. In addition, this model is robust to selection bias issues because any selection characteristics incorporated into the intercepts are controlled for. This approach has three major drawbacks, however; the first drawback is that we lose degrees of freedom when we include state dummy variables, which means that the model produces less efficient estimates of the common slope. The second drawback is that the estimation process[21] wipes out time-invariant explanatory variables. Finally if measurement error is present, it will create more bias with fixed-effects estimators because within-state variation will be heavily contaminated (Kennedy 2003).

In contrast, the random-effects model views the different intercepts

---

[21] This estimation process consists of subtracting from each observation the average of the observations for that state. If the values of a variable are all the same (region, for instance), when we subtract the average, the value becomes zero therefore it is not possible to estimate a slope coefficient for that variable (Kennedy 2003).

as random and treats them as part of the error term. This model therefore estimates an overall intercept, a set of coefficients for variables of interest, and a composite error term (which includes the "random intercept" term measuring the extent to which an individual intercept differs from the overall intercept). The random-effects estimator is more efficient than the fixed-effects estimator for two primary reasons; the first reason is that it is a matrix-weighted average of the between and within estimators, and the second reason is that it saves on degrees of freedom, thereby producing more efficient estimations of the slope coefficients. The random-effects model also permits evaluation of the effects of time-invariant variables such as race, gender, or region, and because it averages variable observations (and averages out the measurement errors), it reduces measurement error bias. It would be tempting to conclude that the random-effects approach is therefore superior to the fixed-effects approach. However, the random-effects model must satisfy one important assumption — namely, for the estimates to be unbiased the unobserved state effects (that give rise to the different intercepts) should be uncorrelated with the other independent variables. If the collective influence of the omitted variables is correlated with the explanatory variables included in the model, omitting them creates bias because the between estimator is biased[22] (Kennedy 2003).

The Hausman (1978) test can detect the presence of this potential bias. It is based on assessing whether the random-effects estimate is insignificantly different from the unbiased fixed-effects estimate. In other words, it is used to test the null hypothesis that random and fixed-effects coefficients are the same, and to assess problems of misspecification in the models. If the Hausman test fails to reject the null, the random-effects estimators are unbiased and should be used since they are more efficient than the fixed-effects estimators. An examination of the full models presented in Chapters 5 and 6 yielded non-significant chi-squared statistics, which indicates that the estimates produced by the random-effects models are unbiased and therefore

---

[22] "The between estimator is biased because a higher x value gives rise to a higher y value, both because x is higher and because the composite error is higher (because the intercept is higher) — the estimating formula gives the change in x all the credit for the change in y." (Kennedy, 2003:307)

more robust and efficient than the estimates obtained with the fixed-effects models. Accordingly, the narrative in the empirical chapters focuses on the results of the random-effects models, but the results from the fixed-effects estimates are also included to show that the results are robust to the two different model specifications.

The general random-effects model is given below in Equation 1:

$$Y_{it} = \alpha + \beta_{yx}X_{it} + \beta_{yz}Z_i + \mu_i + \epsilon_{it} \qquad (1)$$

where Y_{it} is the value of the dependent variable for the ith case in the sample at the tth time period; X_{it} is the vector of time-varying covariates for the ith case at the tth time period; β_{yx} is the row vector of coefficients that give the impact of X_{it} on Y_{it}; Z_i is the vector of observed time-invariant covariates for the ith case with β_{yz} its row vector of coefficients; μ_i is a scalar of all other latent time-invariant variables that influence Y_{it}; and ε_{it} is the random disturbance for the ith case at the tth time period with $\sigma^2_{\varepsilon_t} = \sigma^2_{\varepsilon}$. It also is assumed that ε_{it} is uncorrelated with X_{it}, Z_i, and μ_i. Because time-specific factors can also affect state incarceration/parole revocation numbers, the full model includes a set of dummy variables for each year (Equation 2). These year fixed-effects (δ_t) effectively control for all omitted variables that are invariant across states, yet vary over time.

$$Y_{it} = \alpha + \beta_{yz}X_{it} + \beta_{yz}Z_i + \delta_t + \mu_i + \varepsilon_{it} \qquad (2)$$

Estimation

The dependent variables, the number of people incarcerated (Chapter 5) and number of parole revocations (Chapter 6), are both count variables. Analyzing count data using ordinary linear regression techniques is problematic because linear models are likely to produce nonsensical negative predicted values, and the validity of hypothesis tests in linear regression is based on assumptions about the variance of scores that are unlikely to be met in count data (Gardner et al. 1995). As a result, OLS estimates can be inefficient, inconsistent, and biased (Long 1997). Nonlinear models such as the Poisson and the negative binomial models offer an alternative approach that takes into account the fact that counts are nonnegative, and uses probability distributions for the

                    Penal Sanctioning in the United States

dispersion of the dependent variable scores around the expected value that are appropriate for dependent variables that take on only nonnegative integer values.

Poisson regression is the simplest model for count data, but it is based on two somewhat restrictive assumptions. The first is that events occur independently over time — an assumption unlikely to be valid assumption in the case of penal sanctioning. The second is that the mean of the outcome is equal to the variance; however, in reality the variance often exceeds the mean — a condition referred to as overdispersion (Long 1997; Xekalaki 1983). Using Poisson when overdispersion is present produces underestimated standard errors for the coefficients and overly optimistic significance tests (Cameron and Trivedi 1986). Consequently, Poisson regression should not be used to estimate the probability distributions of the counts for an individual case.

The negative binomial regression addresses concerns about overdispersion by relaxing the assumption of equality between the mean and the variance and including a random component reflecting the uncertainty about the true rates at which events occur for individual cases. In other words, in negative binomial models any variation in the predicted mean is due to both variation in the independent variables across cases and unobserved heterogeneity introduced by an error term. Because more than one mean is possible for each set of observed independent variables, there is a distribution of predicted means rather than a single mean (Long 1997). In addition, the use of exposure, which makes use of the correct probability distributions, is superior to analyzing rates as response variables in many instances (UCLA Statistical Consulting Group).

In the analyses reported here both the Poisson goodness-of-fit tests and the likelihood ratio tests indicate that overdispersion is present and that the Poisson distribution is not appropriate. Accordingly, a random-effects negative binomial regression model is used for testing all hypotheses. Models are estimated using Stata's XTNBREG, RE command with the EXPOSURE option. The exposure is the state population for analyses of incarceration rates (Chapter 5), and the state parole population for analyses of parole revocation rates (Chapter 6). The results of the statistical analyses carried out in these chapters are reported as incidence rate ratios (IRR) rather than as logs of expected counts. Because they include both within-state and between-state effects, the coefficients represent the average effect of X over Y when X changes across time and between states by one unit.

Robustness checks

Because it is likely that it would take one or more years for changes in some structural conditions to influence the outcome variables, the models used in Chapters 5 and 6 specify all independent variables lagged by one year. I conducted additional robustness tests based on alternative model specifications. Specifically, I assessed sensitivity of the results to lags by re-estimating all of the models with two-year lags as well as no lags. Statistical inferences from this sensitivity analysis are almost identical to those presented in the empirical chapters. The results observed in these model replications are quite robust to alternative model specifications.

It is also possible that some variables in the model create an endogeneity problem. One might argue, for example, that crime rates are endogenous to incarceration rates and parole revocation rates, and that the results may be sensitive to this endogeneity bias. To assess this possibility, the tables in Chapters 5 and 6 include models with and without the potentially problematic variables. Thus, Model 5 investigates the effects of symbolic threats, political culture, state governance, sentencing structure, and demographic control variables; Model 6 then adds crime. Results show that statistical inferences remain unchanged; results of Model 6 are not sensitive to the endogeneity of crime.

Chapter 5

Explaining Variations in State-Level Incarceration Rates

INTRODUCTION

In the 1970s the U.S. embarked on a path that resulted in an unprecedented expansion of its correctional system. According to the Bureau of Justice Statistics, state and federal prisons grew by a bewildering 600 percent between 1970 and 2007. In 2005, more than 1.5 million persons were incarcerated in U.S. prisons on any given day, and an additional 750,000 were incarcerated in local jails (Harrison and Beck 2006). By the turn of the twenty-first century, nearly 3 percent of the U.S. population — more than 5.6 million Americans — had served time behind bars (Bonczar 2003), and the incarceration rate had reached 427 inmates per 100,000 residents, up from 87 per 100,000 in 1970.

Within these overall national trends, the numbers producing them reveal a substantial amount of variation in the use of imprisonment among the fifty states. Figure 5.1 demonstrates the extent of this variation by overlapping the range of state incarceration rates for each year onto the national incarceration rate between 1978 and 2007. For example, in 1993 the top of the vertical line represents the state with the highest incarceration rate (about 600 prisoners per 100,000 residents), while the bottom of the line represents the state with the lowest incarceration rate (about 75 prisoners per 100,000 residents). As we can see from the growing range of incarceration rates, state differences in confinement have become greater over time—a reflection of the increasing fragmentation in punishment practices in the states. In addition to variation between states, there is also considerable variation in the rate at which incarceration rates grew *within* states over the last thirty years.

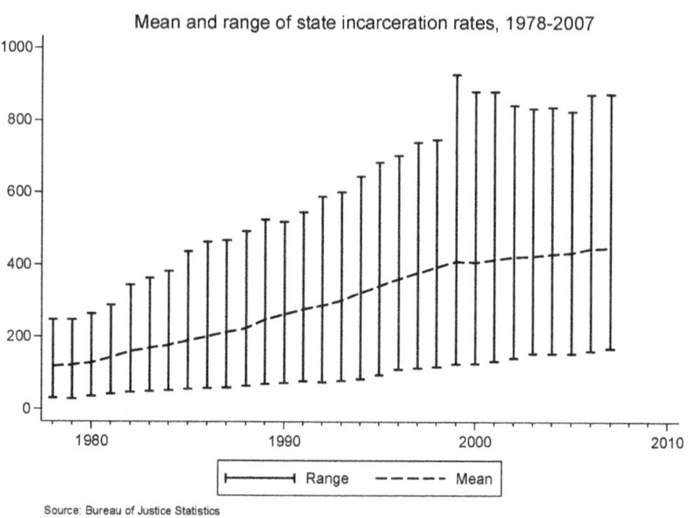

Figure 5.1 Mean and range of state incarceration rates, 1978-2007

In Kentucky, for example, the incarceration rate grew 45 percent between 1971 and 1985, and 190 percent between 1986 and 2002. In contrast, Delaware's increased 745 percent during the first period, but only 60 percent during the next fifteen years (Figure 5.2). Taken together these graphs suggest that, while all states have encountered similar policy problems (increases in crime rates, for instance), they have not pursued the same policy solutions; as a result, the quantitative and qualitative aspects of punishment by incarceration vary significantly from state to state.

What accounts for this patchwork of punishment practices? Empirical research has uncovered several patterns that point to the role of social, political, ideological, economic, policy, and demographic dynamics in shaping state incarceration rates; these studies and their findings are discussed in detail in Chapter 2. However, scholars still struggle to understand the factors behind this state variation and growth, and to come to a consensus about the precise mechanisms through which they come into play. Prior studies suffer from three important limitations; with the exception of some of the more recent longitudinal studies (Spelman 2009; Stemen 2005), they have been limited to short time frames, they tend to focus on a limited number of explanatory variables, and they do not investigate whether the impact of these variables is historically contingent.

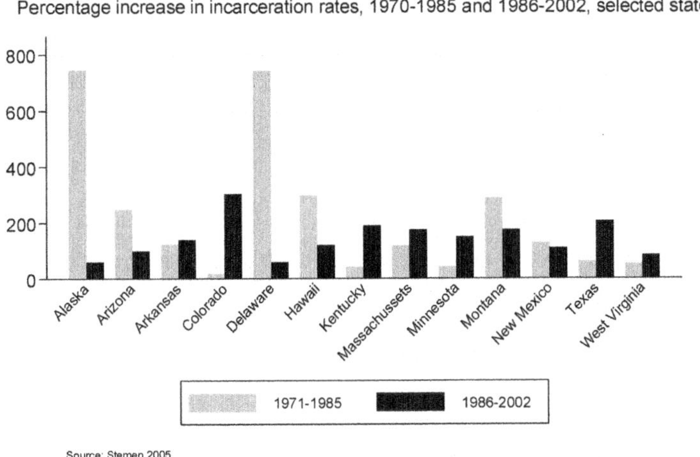

Figure 5.2 Percentage increase in incarceration rates, 1970-85 and 1986-2002, selected states

STUDY GOALS AND HYPOTHESES

This study adds to previous work on the determinants of the size of state prison populations in two important ways. First, it updates the data to consider variation over a longer time frame, extending the analysis to a 30-year period that includes the recent decarceration trend, which studies have yet to examine. By extending the study to 2007 it is hoped that the study may also be able to capture the effects of the economic crisis on incarceration rates, as well as potential course-correction decisions made by the states to keep the size of their prison populations in check after the country's imprisonment binge of the

1980s and 1990s. Second, this study expands the theoretical scope of explanations to include recently developed theories about the role of state governance in shaping punitive practices (Barker 2006).

The study uses pooled time-series cross-sectional (TSCS) data to analyze variations in annual, state-level incarceration rates from 1978 to 2007 — years for which complete and comparable data are available. Building on the work of earlier researchers, various explanations for state differences in incarceration rates that echo long-standing conversations about the determinants of criminal justice outcomes more generally are assessed. Furthermore, this study examine whether the drivers of incarceration rates have changed over time. The data and methods used here are described in detail in Chapter 4, and the modeling strategy adopted is explained in the next section.

The findings from the studies reviewed in Chapter 2 suggest that the determinants of criminal justice outcomes are complex. Accordingly, tests are conducted of the following hypothesized determinants.

Symbolic threats: one of the more widely accepted theories in studies of the rise of mass incarceration is that formal social control in the form of criminalization and incarceration is used as a means to manage populations which present a potential threat to social order. Increases in the size of economically marginalized populations should therefore be associated with increases in incarceration rates (hypothesis 1a). In addition, minority threat theory suggests that the size of minority populations should have an impact on incarceration rates such that there should be a non-linear (inverted U-shaped curve) relationship between percentage Black and incarceration rates (2a), percentage Hispanic should have a positive effect on incarceration rates (2b), and the effect of percentage Hispanic should be smaller than the effect of percentage Black (hypothesis 2c).

Political culture. Based on the number of studies that have uncovered a link between conservative political ideology and harsher stances on punishment, it is expected incarceration rates increase under Republican governors (3a), as well as in states with a more conservative citizenry (3b).

Sentencing structure. The hydraulic displacement of discretion theory proposes that sentencing reforms have transferred sentencing discretion from the judiciary to the legislative branch of government, which has resulted in harsher punishment and higher incarceration rates. Consequently, more limited judicial discretion (as measured by a state's sentencing structure and its parole board authority) should be associated with higher incarceration rates (4).

State governance. Recent scholarship (Barker 2006, 2009) demonstrates that political institutional arrangements and collective agency among citizens provide valuable insights into the different types of penal policies and practices that the states have embraced. Barker suggests, for example, that political structures that create greater centralization of political authority in the state tend to produce a "thin democracy" in which decision-makers are insulated from public demands, resulting in more coercive penal regimes. If that is the case, then the index of gubernatorial power, which is a measure of the centralization of political authority in the state, should be positively associated with incarceration rates (5a). Additionally, civic engagement, meaning the degree to which ordinary citizens get involved in state politics, is likely to influence the nature of the policies created by state political institutions as well as the extent to which states rely on confinement by keeping a check on the repressive powers of the state (Barker 2006). Hence, states with higher levels of civic engagement should have less coercive penal regimes, and by extension lower incarceration rates (hypothesis 5b).

Crime. Tests of the impact of crime on incarceration rates generated mixed results, suggesting that the extent to which states rely on confinement is not entirely determined by a functional response to crime rates. Nonetheless, one cannot ignore the obvious contribution that crime makes to incarceration rates. Therefore, a positive relationship between crime rates and incarceration rates is expected (6).

To further refine this analysis, whether the influence of these factors is historically contingent is investigated. In particular, it is expected that the effects of economic threats (7a), and percentage Hispanic (7b) on incarceration rates become greater over time, while conservative political ideology (8) and crime (9) lose some of their influence.

ANALYSES

Descriptive statistics

The descriptive statistics are reported in Chapter 4 (Table 4.2-4.5), and the intra-class coefficients (ICCs) for all the continuous variables in the analyses are presented here in Table 5.1. The ICC (rho) represents the proportion of the total variance in each variable that is between states. Between-state variance reflects stable differences across states, as opposed to within-state variance which reflects the degree to which values of a given variable change over time.

Most of the variables in Table 5.1 have very high ICCs, which means that the relative ranking of states on these variables did not change very much over time. For example, 99.5 percent of the variance on percent black is between states, meaning any change that occurred over time in this variable did not disrupt the differences between states that were essentially the same at all time periods. Since fixed effects models rely on within-state change over time to estimate the effects of covariates, these results cast doubt on this modeling strategy because there is not sufficient within-state variance on most variables. Interestingly, the dependent variable, incarceration rate, had one of the lower ICCs (.45), which indicates that there was more substantial change over time that could have reshuffled the relative ranking of states on the incarceration rate.

The presence of multicollinearity was investigated because it is often an issue with macrostructural variables; a correlation analysis was carried out in this regard. The results, presented in Table 5.2, show that most associations are quite modest for data aggregated at this level. The strongest bivariate correlation occurred between percentage Black and civic engagement (-0.66).

Table 5-1 Intraclass correlations for all variables in the models

Variables	ICC (rho)
Incarceration rate	0.4465
Crime (standardized index)	0.7425
Economic threat (standardized index)	0.6698
% Black	0.9949
% Hispanic	0.9196
Citizen ideology	0.7801
Civic engagement (standardized index)	0.9153
Gubernatorial power	0.6422
Marriage rate	0.8904
Metropolitan population	0.9206
% 18-24 yr-olds	0.1111

Table 5-2 Pearson's R correlations among covariates, incarceration rates model

	(1)	(2)	(3)	(4)	(5)	(6)	(7)	(8)	(9)	(10)	(11)
Incarceration rate (1)	1.00										
Crime (2)	0.21	1.00									
Economic threat (3)	-0.20	0.15	1.00								
% Black (4)	0.46	0.33	0.29	1.00							
% Hispanic (5)	0.24	0.38	-0.05	-0.13	1.00						
Citizen ideology (6)	-0.12	-0.11	-0.31	-0.19	0.00	1.00					
Civic engagement (7)	-0.34	-0.38	-0.41	-0.66	-0.19	0.23	1.00				
Gubernatorial power (8)	-0.32	-0.00	-0.09	-0.20	-0.11	0.24	0.22	1.00			
Marriage rate (9)	0.06	0.22	-0.03	-0.04	0.07	-0.13	-0.26	-0.14	1.00		
Metropolitan population (10)	0.25	0.49	-0.32	0.24	0.36	0.31	-0.32	0.12	0.05	1.00	
% 18-24 yr-olds (11)	-0.48	0.07	0.43	0.02	-0.17	-0.25	-0.04	0.19	0.03	-0.21	1.00

Basic regression results

Table 5.3 presents the results from the first multivariate analyses carried out. The coefficients are reported as incidence rate ratios (IRR) rather than as logs of expected counts. Because they include both within-state and between-state effects, the coefficients represent the average effect of X on Y when X changes across time and between states by one unit. For ease of interpretation, the expression 100*(IRR-1) tells us the percentage change in the incidence of incarceration (Y) for each unit increase in the independent variable (X). Thus a coefficient of 1.04 for civic engagement in Model 6 means that, controlling for other factors, a one-standard deviation increase in civic engagement is associated with a 6 percent increase in incarceration rates.

As discussed in Chapter 2, pooled time series cross sectional data are typically analyzed using either fixed-effects or random-effects models (Hsiao 1986; Mundlak 1978; Pindyck and Rubinfeld 1991). As noted previously, both procedures have advantages; for example, estimating with the random-effects model allows for the testing of time-invariant explanatory variables and tends to yield more robust and more efficient results, while fixed-effects models ensure that unmeasured effects are not biasing the results. A Hausman test of model specification failed to reject the null hypothesis of "no difference" between the coefficients of the full random- and fixed-effects models (Chi2=26.45, p=.15), which suggests that random-effects estimators should be preferred over fixed-effects estimators. In addition, the relative size of the standard errors in fixed-effects models presents more potential for type I error. Therefore the narrative will focus on the results of the random effects models (Table 5.3 and Table 5.5). This should not be taken to mean that the fixed-effects coefficients are incorrect. As a matter of fact, the results from the fixed-effects models (presented in Table 5.4) show that they yielded remarkably similar results to the random-effects models, thus demonstrating that the results are robust to the different model specifications. Since the models use maximum likelihood estimation, the usual goodness-of-fit parameters are not available. Instead, the Wald chi-squared and the likelihood-ratio chi-squared statistics are reported, which ideally should both decrease as the models get specified further.

Model 1 in Table 5.3 presents the results from the baseline model. This model includes the demographic control variables (marriage, metropolitan population, and percentage 18-24 year-olds), as well as the measures of symbolic threats. The results from model 1 show that economic and racial threat variables each have a non-linear effect on incarceration rates. Specifically, we see from the economic threat coefficients, which are both negative in model 1, that the relationship between economic threat and incarceration is negative (which does not support the research hypothesis) with an accelerating decline as economic threat increases. As predicted, racial and ethnic threats both have a positive impact on incarceration: states with larger Hispanic populations, for example, also have larger prison populations.

Model 2 adds the political explanatory factors (political culture and state governance) to the baseline model. Although they are not significant, the results indicate that the effects (both positive) of Republican governor and gubernatorial power are in the expected direction. Contrary to what was originally hypothesized, citizen ideology[23] and civic engagement are positively associated with incarceration rates (although citizen ideology is not significant). Model 3 tests the effects of sentencing structure. Voluntary guidelines is the only variable that has a statistically significant effect on the size of prison populations; states that have implemented voluntary guidelines have prison populations 9 percent higher than states that have no sentencing guidelines. Model 4 combines the baseline model with the political and sentencing variables. The overall pattern of significance remains unchanged from previous models, except for sentencing variables, where the full parole board authority dummy becomes statistically significant.

Model 5 adds a non-linear effect for time. Controlling for time changes the direction of the effect of a few variables, suggesting that some of the effects estimated in previous models were confounded with general temporal trends across states in incarceration rates. The coefficient for percentage Hispanic, while remaining significant, becomes negatively associated with incarceration rates, as does gubernatorial power. Presumptive guidelines becomes statistically significant, and its effect on prison populations becomes negative.

Finally, crime is added in Model 6 to produce the full analytical model. Adding this variable last allows us to see whether it confounds

---

[23] Citizen ideology is a scale of 0-100, "0" being the most conservative, and "100" being the most liberal.

the effects of other variables in the model. A comparison of the results from Models 5 and 6 shows that the estimates are virtually identical, which indicates that crime measures additional effects not already captured by other variables. As anticipated, the results show a positive, significant (p<0.001) relationship between crime and incarceration rates. However, it is noteworthy that the direction of the rest of the relationships runs contrary to what was expected. The results do not provide much support for advocates of symbolic threat arguments. They indicate that, initially, increases in economic threat lead to higher rates of incarceration, but that after they hit a threshold further increases are associated with declines in incarceration rates. The economic threat hypothesis is supported, but only after controlling for time. Similarly, the coefficients for percentage Black and percentage Hispanic are negative for both, and significant only for percentage Hispanic (p<0.05). Controlling for the other variables in the model, a one percent increase in the Hispanic population is associated with a one percent decrease in incarceration rates. The political affiliation of the governor is not significantly related to incarceration rates (though states with Republican governors do seem to have modestly higher incarceration rates, and greater gubernatorial power seems to have a moderating effect on imprisonment).

The effect of civic engagement continues to be strongly significant; states where ordinary citizens show greater involvement in state politics have higher incarceration rates. Citizen ideology (also positively associated with imprisonment) becomes significant over time, however these effects run contrary to what was hypothesized.

Finally, the results generated from Model 6 indicate that the more structure that is imposed on sentencing both at the front-end and at the back-end, the lower the incarceration rates. It was found that states with parole boards that enjoy full authority over release and revocation decisions have higher incarceration rates compared to states where the authority of the parole board was severely curtailed. Presumptive guidelines, which remove judicial discretion, appear to be associated with lower incarceration rates. This suggests that concerns about the negative effects of sentencing reforms on prison population sizes may be largely unfounded.

Table 5-3 MLE negative binomial regression coefficients (t values) from a series of random effects models of incarceration rates, 1978-2007[a]

Variables[b]	(1) Baseline model	(2) Politics	(3) Sentencing	(4) All	(5) All + time	(6) Full model
Symbolic threats						
Economic threat	0.84*** (-12.70)	0.84*** (-12.67)	0.84*** (-12.63)	0.84*** (-12.71)	1.03* (2.12)	1.02 (1.72)
Economic threat^2	**0.98** (-2.87)	**0.98** (-2.60)	**0.98*** (-3.53)	**0.98** (-3.29)	**0.99** (-2.83)	**0.99*** (-2.09)
(ref=0-2% Black)	.	.	.	.	.	.
2-15% Black	**1.09*** (1.97)	**1.10*** (2.28)	**1.09*** (2.02)	**1.11*** (2.39)	1.00 (-0.05)	0.99 (-0.21)
Over 15% Black	1.06 (1.15)	1.07 (1.35)	1.09 (1.68)	1.10 (1.94)	0.93 (-1.82)	0.94 (-1.57)
% Hispanic	**1.03*** (13.58)	**1.03*** (13.26)	**1.03*** (14.53)	**1.03*** (14.38)	**0.99** (-3.04)	**0.99*** (-2.00)
Demographic variables						
Marriage rate	**1.01*** (4.23)	**1.01*** (4.68)	**1.01*** (4.30)	**1.01*** (4.79)	**1.01*** (7.15)	**1.01*** (7.16)
Metropolitan pop	**0.99*** (-5.06)	**0.99*** (-5.08)	**0.99*** (-4.97)	**0.99*** (-4.96)	**0.99*** (-6.62)	**0.99*** (-7.27)
% 18-24 yr-olds	**0.82*** (-38.47)	**0.82*** (-33.84)	**0.82*** (-37.45)	**0.83*** (-31.89)	**1.04*** (4.26)	**1.03*** (4.07)
Politics						
Citizen ideology		1.00 (-0.43)		1.00 (-0.82)	**1.00*** (-4.23)	**1.00*** (-4.00)
(ref=Dem. governor)		.		.	.	.
Republican governor		1.01 (1.38)		1.02 (1.92)	1.01 (1.31)	1.01 (1.53)
Other governor		0.98 (-0.37)		0.98 (-0.38)	0.96 (-1.17)	0.96 (-1.18)
Civic engagement		**1.04*** (1.97)		**1.05*** (2.53)	**1.05** (3.09)	**1.04** (2.92)
Gubernatorial power		1.01 (0.80)		1.01 (0.62)	0.99 (-1.02)	0.99 (-1.05)

Table 5-3 MLE negative binomial regression coefficients (t values) from a series of random effects models of incarceration rates, 1978-2007[a] (Cond't)

Variables[b]	(1) Baseline model	(2) Politics	(3) Sentencing	(4) All	(5) All + time	(6) Full model
Sentencing structure						
(ref=No PB[c] authority)			.	.	.	.
Limited PB authority			0.96 (-1.24)	0.96 (-1.11)	0.97 (-1.25)	0.98 (-0.77)
Full PB authority			1.05 (1.72)	**1.06**[*] (2.19)	**1.11**[***] (5.46)	**1.11**[***] (5.74)
(ref=No guidelines)						
Voluntary guidelines			**1.09**[***] (3.75)	**1.11**[***] (4.36)	1.03 (1.87)	1.03 (1.44)
Presumpt. guidelines			1.00 (-0.03)	1.02 (0.72)	**0.94**[**] (-2.98)	**0.93**[**] (-3.16)
Time					**1.07**[***] (38.21)	**1.07**[***] (38.37)
Time^2					**1.00**[***] (-20.56)	**1.00**[***] (-18.70)
Crime						**1.03**[***] (4.03)
N	1448	1448	1448	1448	1448	1448
r	4.25	3.91	4.41	3.95	4.06	4.45
s	1672.03	1507.40	1709.04	1493.55	714.55	786.06
Wald chi2	5790.17[***]	5876.15[***]	6019.60[***]	6168.74[***]	10840.87[***]	11027.68[***]
Degrees of freedom	8.00	13.00	12.00	17.00	19.00	20.00
Likelihood ratio chi2	1812.05[***]	1489.71[***]	1707.91[***]	1370.25[***]	1701.82[***]	1565.91[***]

[a] Coefficients are reported as incidence rate ratios.

[b] All variables are lagged by one year.

[c] PB: parole board

[*] $p < 0.05$, [**] $p < 0.01$, [***] $p < 0.001$

Table 5-4 MLE negative binomial regression coefficients (t values) from a series of fixed effects models of incarceration rates, 1978-2007[a]

Variables[b]	(1) Baseline model	(2) Politics	(3) Sentencing	(4) All	(5) All + time	(6) Full model
Symbolic threats						
Economic threat	0.84*** (-12.82)	0.84*** (-12.83)	0.84*** (-12.68)	0 84*** (-12.77)	1.02 (1.66)	1.02 (1.35)
Economic threat^2	**0.98**** (-2.72)	**0.98*** (-2.37)	**0.98**** (-3.37)	**0.98**** (-3.08)	**0.99*** (-2.55)	0.99 (-1.94)
(ref=0-2% Black)	.	.	.	.	.	.
2-15% Black	1.06 (1.25)	1.08 (1.72)	1.06 (1.31)	1.08 (1.86)	0.97 (-0.92)	0.96 (-1.09)
Over 15% Black	1.01 (0.19)	1.03 (0.55)	1.04 (0.72)	1.06 (1.17)	**0.89**** (-2.82)	**0.90**** (-2.65)
% Hispanic	**1.03**** (13.34)	**1.03**** (13.46)	**1.03**** (14.29)	**1.03**** (14.70)	**0.99**** (-3.63)	**0.99**** (-2.67)
Demographic variables						
Marriage rate	**1.01**** (4.57)	**1.01**** (5.21)	**1.01**** (4.74)	**1.01**** (5.41)	**1.01**** (6.68)	**1.01**** (6.72)
Metropolitan pop	**0.99**** (-5.09)	**0.99**** (-5.18)	**0.99**** (-4.89)	**0.99**** (-4.99)	**0.99**** (-7.45)	**0.99**** (-7.98)
% 18-24 yr-olds	**0.82**** (-38.13)	**0.83**** (-33.15)	**0.82**** (-37.13)	**0.83**** (-31.26)	**1.04**** (4.61)	**1.04**** (4.46)
Politics						
Citizen ideology		1.00 (-0.11)		1.00 (-0.55)	**1.00**** (-3.82)	**1.00**** (-3.64)
(ref=Dem. governor)		.		.	.	.
Republican governor		1.01 (1.52)		**1.02*** (2.11)	1.01 (1.35)	1.01 (1.56)
Other governor		0.99 (-0.30)		0.99 (-0.30)	0.96 (-1.18)	0.96 (-1.18)
Civic engagement		**1.06**** (3.06)		**1.08**** (3.62)	**1.06**** (3.66)	**1.05**** (3.55)
Gubernatorial power		1.01 (0.76)		1.01 (0.61)	0.99 (-1.18)	0.99 (-1.18)

Table 5-4 MLE negative binomial regression coefficients (t values) from a series of fixed effects models of incarceration rates, 1978-2007[a] (Cond't)

Variablesb	(1) Baseline model	(2) Politics	(3) Sentencing	(4) All	(5) All + time	(6) Full model
Sentencing structure						
(ref=No PB[c] authority)			.	.	.	.
Limited PB authority			0.96 (-1.20)	0.97 (-0.97)	0.97 (-1.26)	0.98 (-0.85)
Full PB authority			1.05 (1.74)	**1.06**[*] (2.32)	**1.11**[***] (5.26)	**1.11**[***] (5.51)
(ref=No guidelines)						
Voluntary guidelines			**1.09**[***] (3.56)	**1.12**[***] (4.41)	1.02 (1.30)	1.02 (0.97)
Presumptive guidelines			1.00 (0.04)	1.03 (0.95)	**0.93**[**] (-3.23)	**0.93**[***] (-3.35)
Time					**1.07**[***] (38.46)	**1.07**[***] (38.53)
Time^2					**1.00**[***] (-20.46)	**1.00**[***] (-18.81)
Crime						**1.03**[***] (3.40)
N	1448	1448	1448	1448	1448	1448
Wald chi2	5781.95[***]	5881.38[***]	6027.89[***]	6205.37[***]	10728.95[***]	10887.72[***]
Degrees of freedom	8.00	13.00	12.00	17.00	19.00	20.00

[a] Coefficients are reported as incidence rate ratios.

[b] All variables are lagged by one year.

[c] PB: parole board

[*] $p < 0.05$, [**] $p < 0.01$, [***] $p < 0.001$

Estimating period-specific relationships

The results from the first set of models show that several covariates have a strong impact on parole revocations. However, by estimating a single coefficient for the entire 1978 to 2007 period these analyses assume that the strength of these relationships is constant and stable over time, which is <u>not</u> the case; while all states have experienced significant growth in incarceration rates over the last thirty years, this growth has not been uniform over time (Figure 2.1). In addition, as several studies have pointed out (Blumstein and Beck 1999, 2005; Pfaff 2009; Stemen 2005), the factors that gave rise to the prison boom in the 1970s and 1980s are not the same as the factors that sustained its growth in the 1990s, factors which are themselves most certainly different from those that explain the recent decarceration trend. In particular, it is expected that important differences set the 2000s apart, because as the economy has slowed most states have seen their revenues falling. Many have been forced to make tough budgetary decisions and to eliminate or scale back services resulting in prison population reductions in many cases. To explore whether the determinants of incarceration rates are indeed historically contingent, the study was divided into three time periods (1978-1988; 1989-1998; 1999-2007) corresponding to three phases in the growth of incarceration rates; re-estimated Models 2-4 were run for each time period. The results of the periodized models, which appear in Table 5.5, provide strong evidence that the factors responsible for the early build-up in incarceration rates are different from those that have sustained the growth of state prison populations.

Economic and ethnic threats, for example, have an important impact on incarceration rates during the 1980s; the coefficients for these variables are strongly statistically significant ($p<0.001$). However, they appear to affect imprisonment differently. As the first model shows, a one-unit/standard deviation increase in the threat presented by economically marginalized populations is associated with an 11 percent decrease in incarceration rates. This effect is even greater in the 1990s. In contrast, states with larger Hispanic populations have higher incarceration rates. Percentage Hispanic becomes negatively associated with imprisonment during the 1990s, but the coefficient fails to achieve statistical significance. The relationship becomes positive and significant again during the 2000s. The positive relationship between racial threats and incarceration rates carries through all three periods, but it becomes significant only in the last decade, when states where over 15 percent of the population is Black have 10 percent higher incarceration rates compared to states with very small (0 to 2 percent) Black populations ($p<0.05$).

The models show that, through most of the 30 years, states with a more liberal citizenry have higher incarceration rates. Although this effect is very small, it is statistically significant and it is at odds with the influence of Republican governor; this coefficient shows that, compared to states with Democratic governors, states with Republican governors have higher incarceration rates in the 1980s (which we would expect), but lower incarceration rates in the 1990s. The relationship becomes non-significant and virtually indistinguishable from zero during the 2000s, which suggests that political differences may have disappeared when it comes to backing strong crime control legislation and that partisanship is no longer a good predictor of harsh stances on punishment. The influence of civic engagement does not become significant ($p<0.001$) until the last decade. Greater gubernatorial power is associated with lower incarceration rates initially, but the relationship changes sign in the 1990s when a one-unit increase in this covariate is related to an 11 percent increase in incarceration rates.

The models indicate that states achieve lower incarceration rates differently in the different periods. During the 1980s, states that exerted more control over releases (through determinate sentencing) had significantly lower incarceration rates. Controlling admissions (through the use of presumptive guidelines) had the opposite effect, but this coefficient is not statistically significant. However, it is the combination of determinate sentencing and presumptive guidelines that has the largest effect on incarceration rates. During the 1990s, it appears that the opposite happened — that is, incarceration rates are affected negatively by presumptive guidelines, and positively by determinate sentencing. The relationship between the combination of determinate sentencing and presumptive guidelines, and incarceration rates is positive, but this coefficient is not statistically significant. The influence of sentencing factors all but disappears during the first decade of the twenty-first century, when only determinate sentencing has a significant (negative) impact on incarceration rates.

Table 5-5 MLE negative binomial regression coefficients (t values) from a series of models of incarceration rates stratified by time period, 1978-2007[a]

Variables[b]	(1) 1978-1988	(2) 1989-1998	(3) 1999-2007
Symbolic threats			
Econ. threat	**0.89***** (-5.51)	**0.88***** (-6.29)	1.02 (1.28)
(ref=0-2% Black)	.	.	.
2-15% Black	0.92 (-1.21)	1.09 (1.00)	1.05 (1.43)
> 15% Black	1.13 (1.54)	1.05 (0.57)	**1.10*** (2.35)
% Hispanic	**1.04***** (7.58)	0.99 (-1.09)	**1.01*** (2.51)
Demographic variables			
Marriage rate	**1.01***** (4.21)	1.00 (0.14)	1.00 (1.08)
Metro pop	1.00 (0.06)	1.00 (0.84)	**1.00*** (2.53)
% 18-24 yr-olds	**0.85***** (-12.61)	**0.82***** (-14.52)	1.01 (1.41)
Politics			
Citizen ideology	1.00 (1.53)	**1.00***** (-3.32)	**1.00**** (2.83)
(ref=Dem. gov.)	.	.	.
Republican gov.	**1.09***** (6.44)	**0.97*** (-2.00)	1.00 (0.53)
Other governor	0.81 (-0.63)	0.97 (-0.71)	**0.85***** (-4.58)
Civic engagement	1.03 (1.12)	0.98 (-0.94)	**1.06***** (3.68)
Gubernatorial power	**0.91***** (-3.71)	**1.11**** (3.01)	1.00 (0.05)
Sentencing structure			
(ref=No PB[c] authority)	.	.	.
Limited PB authority	**1.43**** (2.65)	0.89 (-1.90)	**0.89**** (-2.76)
Full PB authority	**1.37***** (6.66)	**0.85***** (-3.89)	0.95 (-1.25)
(ref=No guidelines)			
Voluntary guidelines	1.07 (1.79)	**0.89**** (-2.76)	1.00 (-0.08)
Presumptive guid.	**1.25***** (4.78)	**0.89*** (-2.43)	0.97 (-0.96)
Crime	**0.87***** (-6.40)	**0.94***** (-3.48)	1.00 (0.14)
N	498	500	450
r	3.50	3.42	6.10
s	312.06	584.49	330.12
Wald chi2	1362.58***	773.35***	117.62***
Degrees of freedom	17.00	17.00	17.00
Likelihood ratio chi2	426.73***	537.29***	960.73***

[a] Coefficients are reported as incidence rate ratios.

[b] All variables are lagged by one year.

[c] PB: parole board

* $p < 0.05$, ** $p < 0.01$, *** $p < 0.001$

The effect of crime is unexpected. Indeed, the models show that, contrary to what other studies have found, there is a negative relationship between crime and incarceration rates in the 1980s and 1990s. The coefficients, strongly significant, indicate that an increase in crime is associated with a 13 percent decrease in incarceration rates in the 1980s, and a 6 percent decrease in the 1990s. Only in the last ten-year period does the relationship become positive.

In summary, the results show that, although they did not all have the anticipated effects, crime, symbolic threats, political culture, and sentencing reforms were all important determinants of incarceration rates in the 1980s. During this period, incarceration rates were driven up by ethnic threats, political factors, and sentencing factors, and down by crime and economic threats. In the 1990s incarceration rates continue to be driven by crime, economic threats, political culture, and sentencing factors. Racial and ethnic threats do not appear to have an influence on the size of state prison populations. In addition, with the exception of gubernatorial power, most of the covariates are negatively associated with imprisonment during this period. These relationships shift again in the third period, when citizen ideology, and racial and ethnic threats are associated with increases in incarceration rates. Civic engagement emerges as an important factor also.

DISCUSSION AND WIDER IMPLICATIONS

Summary of main findings

The goal of this chapter was to examine the factors that drive incarceration rates and to explore whether these relationships are historically contingent. I relied on major findings from the criminological literature to construct and test a series of hypotheses using thirty years of aggregate data on all fifty American states.

At first glance most of the results appear consistent with patterns uncovered in previous studies of the determinants of incarceration rates. For instance, it comes as no surprise that incarceration rates increase with crime, symbolic threats, or in response to sentencing reforms or practical constraints. The relationship between crime and incarceration is, after all, partly a mechanical one: "Imprisonment is a criminal sanction: its use will therefore fluctuate in direct proportion to changes in the level of the behavior to which it is designed to respond" (Zimring and Hawkins 1991: 121). But the results from the periodized analyses suggest a considerably more complex relationship. According to these models, crime is associated with *lower* incarceration rates in the 1980s and 1990s, and higher incarceration rates in the 2000s. It may be, as some authors have argued (Tonry 1999), that the relationship between crime and incarceration rates is not as much about changes in crime rates as it is about persistently high crime rates shaping public attitudes about punishment (in turn affecting prison populations). If this is true, then the impact of crime may have a lag effect. Perhaps that would explain why crime rates are positively associated with confinement in the 2000s even after they peaked in the mid-1990s (Figure 2.5). The economic difficulties associated with the recent collapse of financial markets are reminiscent of the recessions of the 1970s (unemployment, increasing precariousness of the labor market, threat of inflation) and may also explain why both crime and economic threat become positively associated with incarceration rates in the third period.

Critics of sentencing reforms have argued that the adoption of limiting enactments, sentencing guidelines, and mandatory sentencing laws may have contributed to increases in incarceration rates by mandating that harsher penalties be imposed on defendants, and by limiting the system's ability to respond to overcrowding because it is now locked into inflexible policies (at the front end and at the back end). Unable to use sentencing as an informal means of controlling the size of prison populations, the argument goes, many states have been placed under court orders to relieve overcrowding, as Michigan was after the 1981 Overcrowding Emergency Powers Act was passed. The findings of this study provide little evidence in support of this argument. Generally speaking, incarceration rates *are* responsive to changes in sentencing policies, but not in the way that is commonly anticipated. Indeed, the results show that it is states that exercise *greater* control over admissions and over releases that have lower incarceration rates, a result similar to what Stemen and his colleagues found (2005). Far from contributing to the growth of prison populations, then, curtailing judicial discretion seems to have had a moderating effect on incarceration rates increases. However, it is important to note that the results from the periodized analyses suggest that this is not entirely true. The findings are consistent with previous research showing that sentencing practices, rather than changes in criminal behavior, were responsible for the early build-up of the prison boom; for example, sentencing variables have particularly strong effects in the 1980s. However, the periodized analyses paint a complex picture. During this period, states that exercised *greater control* over prison admissions through the implementation of sentencing guidelines had as much as 25 percent *higher* incarceration rates compared to states that did not. Initially then, sentencing guidelines did contribute to the prison boom. Meanwhile, *lesser control* over releases (i.e., more parole board discretion) was associated with (about 40 percent) *higher* incarceration rates, an indication perhaps that parole boards responded to the sustained attacks on parole and the toughening of stances on criminals in the political culture by becoming considerably more conservative in their willingness to grant early release. This all changed in the 1990s, when structured sentencing and greater parole board authority are both associated with lower incarceration rates.

The periodization models provide no easy answer for this turnabout. It is possible that, upon seeing the effects of sentencing reforms on prison population sizes and correctional budgets during the previous decade, states started reframing their sentencing guidelines from tough-on-crime measures to population reduction measures (Kramer 1992; Marvell 1995; Nicholson-Crotty 2004). The finding that discretion appears to work in opposite directions at the front end and at the back end of the system also merits considerable further exploration.

Surprisingly, the results provide little support for the symbolic threats arguments that incarceration is used as a means of controlling marginal classes and preserving social order (Wacquant 2005). Indeed, generally speaking, prisons were *smaller* in states where economically marginalized populations and racial and ethnic groups were larger. Neither is there any evidence that there exists a non-linear, inverted U-shaped effect of racial populations on criminal justice outcomes, as some have claimed (Keen and Jacobs 2009). An inverted U-shaped relationship would indicate that criminal sanctioning increases with the size of Black populations, until this population reaches a certain threshold at which point sanctioning becomes less severe. Scholars have speculated that the extent to which Black populations are perceived as "threatening" is tied to their voting power: once this demographic becomes a large enough voting segment of the population, the argument goes, it is able to influence lawmakers and weaken the policies that produce racial disparities in the criminal justice system. The same (albeit with different thresholds) may be true of Hispanics, whose vote both sides of the political spectrum increasingly need in order to get elected. The findings of this study do show that the impact of percentage Black is not linear, but it does not take the form of an inverted U, and the direction of the effect is highly contingent on the period under consideration.

The findings also refute the argument that race affects criminal justice outcomes, but ethnicity does not. As a matter of fact, in the full model (Table 5.3), as well as in two of the periods (Table 5.5), the coefficient for percentage Hispanic is significant but that of percentage Black is not. The effect of percentage Hispanic tends to be weaker however, which is consistent with the argument that the two groups enjoy a different status in the U.S. racial and ethnic hierarchy, where "Blacks have long been perceived as so physically and culturally different from Whites to warrant a separate 'racial' category both in the public mind and the legal sphere" (Dixon 2006, 2184; see also Muhammad 2010) but Hispanics are perceived as culturally assimilated, and therefore less threatening than Blacks. The perception that this group constitutes a lesser "threat" could be compounded by the fact that, until recently, Hispanics represented a small minority of the U.S. population, and the recent sharp growth of the Hispanic population should lead to a stronger coefficient in the last decade of the periodized models. Surprisingly, this is not the case: percentage Hispanic is statistically significant and positively associated with incarceration rates in the 2000s, but its effect is more modest than it was during the 1980s, when a one percentage point increase in the size of Hispanic populations was associated with a 4 percent increase in incarceration rates. Further studies may need to explore the possibility that regional subcultures and political economies mediate the impact of this variable.

Another interesting finding concerns the "dog that did not bark," to borrow a phrase from Arthur Conan Doyle. Many studies have shown that the Republican Party and conservative political values produce increases, as well as faster growth, in the prison population (Jacobs and Carmichael 2001; Jacobs and Helms 1999). However, the results of the general models show that the political party of governor fails to make a significant contribution to incarceration rates, which would support Greenberg and West's (2001) contention that "the political incentives for an expansive prison policy transcend party affiliations" (638). The periodized models indicate that this too is a bit of an oversimplification, however. The influence of Republican governors over incarceration rates became weaker over the period; it exerted a strong influence over incarceration rates in the 1980s when the Republican Party led the calls for law and order, but actually became negatively associated with imprisonment in the 1990s, and became insignificant in the 2000s. As for citizen ideology, it seems to have a very small, but significant and positive impact on incarceration rates. In other words, states with a more liberal citizenry have larger prison populations, a finding which is unexpected. Equally as surprising is the effect of civic engagement. Barker's (2006) assertion is that differences in the democratic process — i.e. to structures of state governance and practices of civic engagement — explain why American states use punishment and confinement differently. Her comparative study of the states of California, New York, and Washington found that widespread civic engagement tends to moderate states' use of harsh punishments, and that the centralization of political authority works to insulate the state from public demands and to lead to a differentiated use of punishment. My results provide only mixed support for her arguments. They show instead that states with greater centralization of political authority (as measured by the index of gubernatorial power) have lower incarceration rates, but only in the 1980s. The effect of civic engagement, similarly, is less straightforward than suggested. This factor has a significant, positive impact on incarceration rates in the general model and in the 2000s, but Barker's assertion about the moderating role of civic engagement on state's punitive practices is only true during the 1990s. It is possible that citizen ideology mediates the effects of civic engagement, but it is difficult to gauge from these models the precise mechanisms through which civic engagement affects punishment practices. Nevertheless, the results suggest that Barker is correct in drawing our attention to the importance of exploring differences in state democratic processes and articulating better models of the influence of state governance on criminal justice outcomes. Such work is empirically beyond the scope of the current study, but is likely necessary to fully understand states' differentiated use of penal sanctioning.

Taken together, the period-specific results provide some insights into the dynamics of mass imprisonment in the U.S. over the last 30 years. They show that ethnic threats, the strength of the Republican party, as well as sentencing practices were largely responsible for the early build-up in incarceration rates in the 1980s, but actually moderated their growth in the 1990s, a decade during which the drivers of prison populations shifted toward citizen ideology and state modes of governance. This trend continued into the 2000s when symbolic threats also became an important determinant of incarceration rates.

Wider implications

The findings demonstrate the complex nature of penal policymaking. From a theoretical perspective, they support the continuing utility of considering those factors identified in the literature as significant drivers of criminal punishment practices in late modern American society. But they also indicate that the importance of some of these factors may have been overstated. In particular, the results of this study lend surprisingly little support for the influence of conservative ideology on incarceration rates, and suggest that differences in the scope of penal sanctioning may be better understood through the lens of varying political institutional contexts and practices of civic engagement instead. This is a promising avenue of investigation, but better models are needed that conceptualize and operationalize these variables more carefully. Finally, the results show that these various relationships need to be examined within their historical context if we are to understand how we have arrived at such a patchwork of punishment practices in the American states.

From a policy perspective, the findings help to alleviate concerns over the negative impact of sentencing reforms, which have been said to dehumanize the sentencing process and increase commitment and incarceration rates. Indeed, the results reported here show that while the intent behind limiting enactments may have been to produce harsh punishments by curbing judicial discretion, in practice they have not necessarily resulted in higher incarceration rates. As a matter of fact, it is states that exercise tight control over both admissions and releases (in other words, they curb discretion at the front end and at the back end) that have lower incarceration rates. This suggests that we need to revisit the criticisms leveled against grid-based sentencing schemes because they may present a valuable opportunity to achieve meaningful long-term changes in punishment patterns.

Chapter 6

Investigating Back-door Prison Intake: An Analysis of Parole Revocation Rates

INTRODUCTION

The landscape of criminal punishment has changed dramatically in the United States over the last forty years, and nowhere in the criminal justice system have these changes been felt more acutely than in the area of corrections. Incarceration rates have soared, propelled initially (in the 1970s and 80s) by crime trends, increased prosecutorial effectiveness and tougher judicial sanctioning, and subsequently by changes in sentencing policies and practices (such as three-strikes and truth-in-sentencing laws) that lengthened time served at the front end and increased parole revocations at the back end (Blumstein and Beck 2005; Langan 1991; Sabol et al. 2002).

This increase in parole revocations is significant. While the overall prison population increased fourfold between 1980 and 2000, the number of parolees revoked and recommitted grew *sevenfold* — from 27,000 in 1980 (or 17 percent of prison admissions nationally), to 133,900 in 1990, and 232,000 in 2005 (or 36 percent of all admissions) — far outstripping the overall growth in incarceration (Blumstein and Beck 2005; Glaze and Palla 2005; McBride 2009; Travis 2005) (Figure 6.1). Scholars now estimate that back-end sentencing (the decision to revoke parole and recommit) has been *the* dominant factor in the incarceration rate increases we have seen in the last 20 years, accounting for as much as 60 percent of the growth in the nation's prison population between 1990 and 2001 (Blumstein and Beck 2005).

Parole violators thus make up a substantial percentage of prison inmates in all states, and revocations contribute to the phenomenon of "churning" in which offenders circulate in and out of custody repeatedly — a problematic trend that stresses state resources and is being criticized as largely counterproductive because it destabilizes families, weakens communities, and generally speaking makes no sense in terms of deterrence, incapacitation, treatment or cost (Clear 2007; Manza and Uggen 2006; Western 2006).

Figure 6.1 State prison population and parole revocations, 1978-2007[24]

These overall national statistics paint a worrisome picture, and reveal important trends while also hiding considerable state-level variation (Figure 6.2). For example, a National Institute of Corrections study of parole violations and prison admissions in Georgia, Kansas, New Jersey and Rhode Island found that revocation rates in these four states ranged from 20 to 60 percent (Burke 2004). Figure 6.3 illustrates the trends in parole revocation rates in these states. It shows that while

---

[24] For a discussion of the two "dips" in parole revocation rates in 1991 and 1993, see Appendix B.

they all had similar parole revocation rates in the late 1970s, by the year 2000 parolees in Kansas were getting revoked at four times the rate of parolees in Georgia. This suggests that while parole revocations contribute to incarceration rates in all states, the extent of this contribution is much greater in some states than in others.

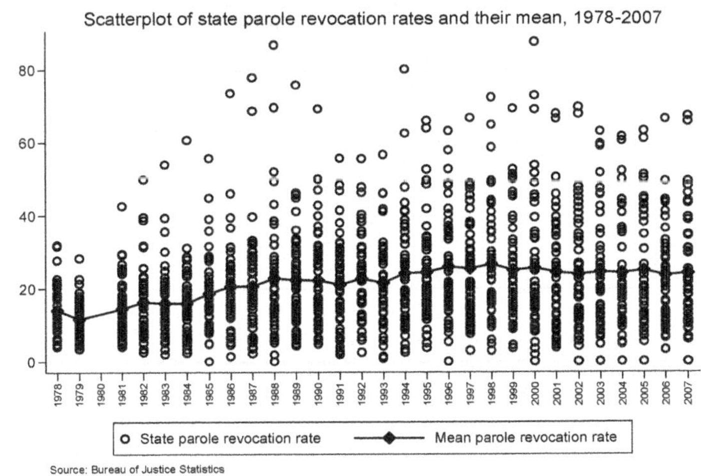

Figure 6.2 Scatterplot of state parole revocation rates and their mean, 1978-2007

As Figure 6.4 shows, parole revocations now account for over 60 percent of prison admissions in California, but only 10 percent in Rhode Island. This begs the question, why? If parolees tend to violate the conditions of their parole at similar rates in all states, why do states have widely different rates of parole revocations? What factors explain these discrepancies, and what do they tell us about the meaning of parole revocation as a sanction, and about the role of parole in the development of the American carceral state?

Scholars have noted the significant contribution of parole violations to the unprecedented growth of the U.S. prison system over the last four decades, yet little is known about its determinants. The complex factors that shape parole revocation policies and practices at the state level — as well as their consequences for prisoners' reentry

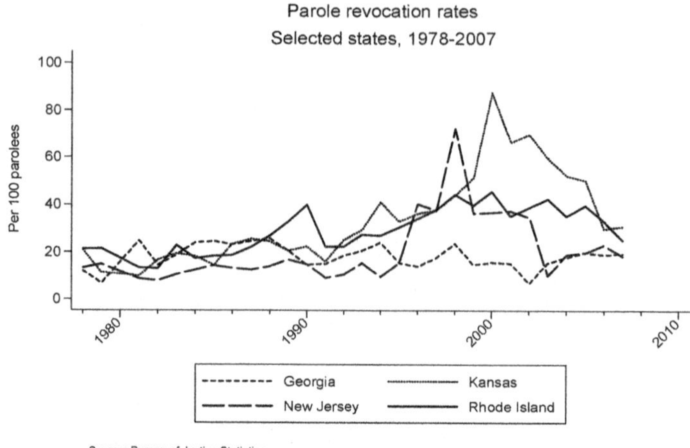

Figure 6.3 Parole revocation rates, selected states, 1978-2007

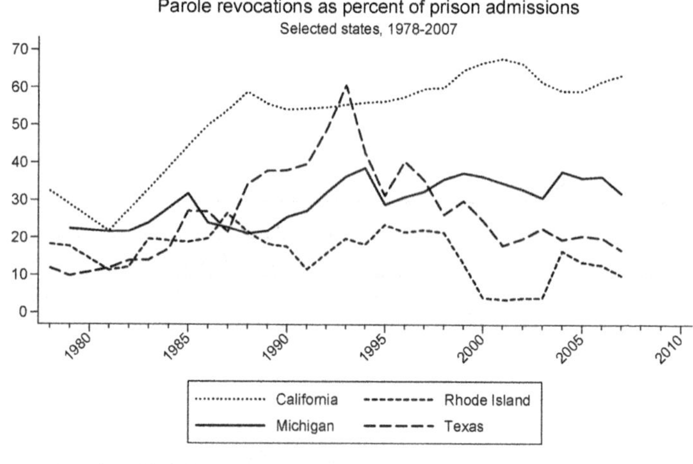

Figure 6.4 Parole revocations as percentage of prison admissions, selected states, 1978-2007

success, prison populations, costs, and public safety — have received little scrutiny in the sociological literature (a surprising fact given the social, political, and economic impact of bulging prisons). In particular, criminologists have yet to explore whether the factors driving incarceration rates also apply to the specific mechanisms of parole revocation and to provide a rigorous treatment of criminal justice system responses to violations. Parole occupies a unique position within the criminal justice system: on the one hand, back-end sentencing (despite often being overlooked by modern sentencing jurisprudence and punishment theory) is an integral dimension of the criminal justice system that shares conceptual and operational characteristics with front-end sentencing. As such, one would expect it to be subject to the same macro-level processes that impact the system as a whole. On the other hand, back-end sentencing stands apart from the rest of the system in that it involves a different set of actors who operate according to different rules, with limited exposure to public and judicial scrutiny. Given these differences it may not be influenced by the same factors, or perhaps not in the same manner, as other aspects of the criminal justice system.

STUDY GOALS AND HYPOTHESES

The goal of this aspect of the study set forth here is to fill this gap in the criminological literature by using pooled time-series cross-sectional (TSCS) data to analyze variations in annual, state-level revocation rates from 1978 to 2007, years for which complete and comparable data are available[25]. By extending the study to 2007 (the most recent year for which we might reasonably expect to find complete data), it was hoped that the study may also be able to capture the effects of the economic crisis on parole revocation decisions, as well as potential course-correction decisions made by the state legislatures to keep the size of their prison populations in check after the country's imprisonment binge of the 1980s and 1990s.

---

[25] 1978 was chosen as the cut-off year because, while 1975 ushered in many significant changes in state-level sentencing and corrections policies, the Bureau of Justice Statistics (BJS) did not start compiling systematic, detailed data on revocation until the mid-80s (National Corrections Reporting Program). Therefore it is difficult to find reliable revocation data sources pre-1978.

Specifically, various explanations for state differences in parole revocation rates that echo long-standing conversations about the determinants of criminal justice outcomes more generally are assessed. Furthermore, whether the drivers of parole revocations have changed over time is examined. The data and methods used are described in detail in Chapter 4, and the modeling strategy is explained in the next section.

The empirical patterns uncovered by the studies reviewed in Chapter 2 and Chapter 3 suggest that the determinants of criminal justice outcomes are complex. Accordingly, tests of the following set of hypotheses are conducted.

Symbolic threats: one of the more widely accepted theories in studies of the rise of mass incarceration is that formal social control in the form of criminalization and incarceration is used as a means to manage populations which present a potential threat to social order. "Social deregulation, the rise of precarious wage work ... and the return of an old-style punitive state go hand in hand," Wacquant argues, "the invisible 'hand' of the casualised labour market finds its counterpart in the 'iron fist' of the state which is being redeployed as to check the disorders generated by the diffusion of social insecurity" (2001: 401). Increases in the size of economically marginalized populations should therefore be associated with increases in parole revocation rates (hypothesis 1a). In addition, minority threat theory suggests that the size of minority populations should have an impact on parole revocation rates such that there should be a non-linear (inverted U-shaped curve) relationship between percentage Black and parole revocation rates (2a); percentage Hispanic should have a positive effect on parole revocation rates (2b); and the effect of percentage Hispanic should be smaller than the effect of percentage Black (hypothesis 2c).

Political culture. Based on the number of studies that have uncovered a link between conservative political ideology and harsher stances on punishment, it is expected that parole revocation rates increase under Republican governors (3a), as well as in states with a more conservative citizenry (3b).

Sentencing structure. The hydraulic displacement of discretion theory proposes that sentencing reforms have transferred sentencing discretion from the judiciary to the legislative branch of government, a transfer of authority which has resulted in harsher punishment and higher incarceration rates. More limited judicial discretion (as measured by a state's sentencing structure and its parole board authority) should also be associated with higher parole revocation rates (4).

State governance. Recent scholarship (Barker 2006, 2009) demonstrates that political institutional arrangements and collective agency among citizens provide valuable insights into the different types of penal policies and practices that the states have embraced. Barker suggests, for example, that political structures that create greater centralization of political authority in the state tend to produce a "thin democracy" in which decision-makers are insulated from public demands, resulting in more coercive penal regimes. If that is the case, then the index of gubernatorial power, which is a measure of the centralization of political authority in the state, should be positively associated with parole revocation rates (5a). Additionally, civic engagement — the degree to which ordinary citizens get involved in state politics — is likely to influence the nature of the policies created by state political institutions, as well as the extent to which states rely on confinement, by keeping a check on the repressive powers of the state (Barker 2006). Hence, it follows that states with higher levels of civic engagement should have less coercive penal regimes, and by extension lower parole revocation rates (hypothesis 5b).

Crime. Although tests of the impact of crime on incarceration rates have been met with mixed results, one cannot ignore the obvious contribution that crime makes to incarceration rates. Similarly, one would expect that states attempt to address concerns over rising crime rates by cracking down on parole violations and increasing the number of parole revocations (6).

Practical constraints. We might also expect a state's ability to implement punitive policies to be tied to its economic health and the availability of human and logistical resources. The smaller the share of corrections in the state budget, the fewer resources can be devoted to the detection and sanctioning of parole violations (hypothesis 7).

To further refine this analysis, I also investigate whether the relationships between these various factors and parole revocation rates are historically contingent. In particular, I expect to find that the effects of economic threats (8a), and percentage Hispanic (8b) on parole revocations become greater over time, while conservative political ideology (9) and crime (10) lose some of their influence over time.

ANALYSES

Descriptive statistics

The descriptive statistics are reported in Chapter 4 (Table 4.2- 4.5). Table 6.1 shows the intra-class coefficients (ICCs) for all the continuous variables in the models. The ICC (rho) represents the proportion of the total variance in each variable that is between states. Between-state variance reflects stable differences across states, as opposed to within-state variance which reflects the degree to which values of a given variable change over time. Most of the variables in Table 6.1 have very high ICCs, which means that the relative ranking of states on these variables did not change very much over time. For example, 99.5 percent of the variance on percentage black is between states, meaning any change that occurred over time in this variable did not disrupt the differences between states that were essentially the same at all time periods. Since fixed-effects models rely on within-state change over time to estimate the effects of covariates, these results cast doubt on this modeling strategy because there is not sufficient within-state variance on most variables.

Table 6-1 Intraclass correlations (ICCs) for all variables in the models of parole revocations

Variables	ICC (rho)
Parole revocations	0.8002
Crime (standardized index)	0.7425
Economic threat (standardized index)	0.6698
% Black	0.9949
% Hispanic	0.9196
Citizen ideology	0.7801
Corrections (standardized index)	0.4935
Civic engagement (standardized index)	0.9153
Gubernatorial power	0.6422
Marriage rate	0.8904
Metropolitan population	0.9206
% 18-24 yr-olds	0.1111

Because multicollinearity among predictor variables is often an issue with macrostructural variables, a correlation analysis was performed. The results of this analysis, presented in Table 6.2, show that at -0.66, the strongest bivariate correlation occurred between percentage Black and civic engagement.

Basic regression results

The first multivariate analyses are reported in Table 6.3. Note that the coefficients are reported as incidence rate ratios (IRR) rather than as logs of expected counts. Because they include both within-state and between-state effects, the coefficients represent the average effect of X on Y when X changes across time and between states by one unit. For ease of interpretation, the expression 100*(IRR-1) tells us the percentage change in the incidence of parole revocation (Y) for each unit increase in the independent variable (X); for example, the coefficient for civic engagement is 1.30 in Table 6.3, Model 4. This indicates that a one standard deviation increase in civic engagement is associated with a 30 percent increase in parole revocations.

As discussed in Chapter 4, pooled time-series cross-sectional data are typically analyzed using either fixed-effects or random-effects models (Hsiao 1986; Mundlak 1978; Pindyck and Rubinfeld 1991). Both procedures have their respective advantages; for example, estimating with random-effects allows for the testing of time-invariant explanatory variables and tends to yield more robust and more efficient results, while fixed-effects models ensure that unmeasured effects are not biasing the results. A Hausman test of model specification failed to reject the null hypothesis of "no difference" between the coefficients of the random- and fixed-effects models (chi2=30.97, p=.078) generated in this analysis.

In addition, since the relative size of the standard errors in fixed-effects models presents more potential for type I error, the narrative focuses on the results of the random-effects models (Table 6.3). This is not to say that the fixed-effects coefficients are incorrect. As a matter of fact, the fixed-effects models (presented in Table 6.4) and random-effects models (presented in Table 6.3) yielded remarkably similar estimates, an outcome which demonstrates that the results are robust to the different model specifications.

Since the models use maximum likelihood estimation, the usual goodness-of-fit parameters are not available. Instead, the Wald chi-squared and the likelihood-ratio chi-squared statistics are reported which ideally should both decrease as the models get specified further.

Model 1 in Table 6.3 presents the results from the baseline model. This model includes the demographic control variables (marriage, metropolitan population, and percentage 18-24 year-olds), as well as the measures of symbolic threats. The results confirm that economic and racial threat variables have a non-linear effect on incarceration rates. Specifically, we see from the economic threat coefficients that the effect of economic threats follows a U-shape; the coefficient of the linear term is negative, indicating that parole revocations initially decrease as economic threats increase, but the positive coefficient for the quadratic shows that as levels of economic threat increase further, parole revocations increase as well. This finding does not support the research hypothesis. Neither is the influence of racial and ethnic threats as anticipated, since these coefficients are negative. States with larger Black populations have lower parole revocation rates. This effect diminishes somewhat when Black populations reach 15 percent, as the modestly smaller coefficient indicates. The results, therefore, confirm a non-linear effect, but show no evidence that it takes the form of an inverted U-shape.

Model 2 adds the political explanatory factors (political culture and state governance) to the baseline model. Although it is not significant, the results indicate that the effect (positive) of Republican governor is in the expected direction. However the effects of citizen ideology, civic engagement and gubernatorial power are not. Contrary to what was hypothesized, parole revocations are negatively affected by gubernatorial power, and positively (and significantly, in the case of civic engagement) impacted by citizen ideology and civic engagement. Model 3 tests the effects of sentencing structure. The coefficients for parole board authority and sentencing guidelines are all strongly statistically significant, but they do not support the research hypothesis that greater discretion would be associated with lower parole revocation rates. In fact, the results show precisely the opposite — that is, states whose parole boards have retained full authority have revocation rates 18 percent *higher* than states that have abolished their parole board.

For example, states that have implemented presumptive guidelines (which constrain discretion the most) have revocation rates 17 percent *lower* than states with no sentencing guidelines at all.

Model 4 combines the baseline model with the political and sentencing variables. The overall patterns of significance remain unchanged from previous models. Model 5 adds a non-linear effect for time. With the exception of percentage Hispanic, which becomes negative and statistically significant, controlling for time does not alter the overall significance patterns of most variables in the model whose coefficients remain virtually unaffected in both size and direction.

This finding suggests that the effects estimated in previous models were not confounded with general temporal trends across states in parole revocation rates. Finally crime and corrections are added in Model 6 to produce the full model. Adding these variables last allows us to see whether they confound the effects of other variables in the model. A comparison of the results from Models 5 and 6 shows that the estimates are virtually identical, which indicates that crime and the corrections index measure effects not already captured by other variables.

Core findings from Model 6 show that the associations between crime, symbolic threats, and political factors on the one hand, and parole revocations on the other, are negative for the most part, which fails to support several of the research hypotheses. Thus, while the coefficient for crime fails to achieve statistical significance, it suggests that an increase in crime is associated with lower levels of parole revocations. Similarly, arguments about the effects of economic and racial threats appear unsupported, as the results indicate that greater levels of both types of threats are significantly related to fewer parole revocations. In the case of racial threats, the results show that parole revocations decrease at a slower pace as percentage Black increases over 15 percent. The size of Hispanic populations does not appear to have much of an effect at all.

Considering the number of studies that have linked a conservative political ideology with harsher stances on punishment, it is surprising to see here that the effect of citizen ideology on parole revocations is virtually non-existent, and that not only is the effect of Republican governor not significant, but it is also negative in direction. Greater civic engagement, on the other hand, has a strong, positive impact on parole revocations: a one standard deviation increase in this index is associated with a 33 percent increase in parole revocations ($p<0.001$). This finding suggests that the degree to which ordinary citizens get involved in state politics does *not* work to keep a check on the repressive power of the state, contrary to what has been hypothesized here and elsewhere (Barker 2006).

Table 6-2 Pearson's R correlations among covariates, parole revocation models

	(1)	(2)	(3)	(4)	(5)	(6)	(7)	(8)	(9)	(10)	(11)
Parole revocations (1)	1.00										
Crime (2)	0.13	1.00									
Economic threat (3)	-0.06	0.15	1.00								
% Black (4)	0.04	0.33	0.29	1.00							
% Hispanic (5)	0.48	0.38	-0.05	-0.13	1.00						
Citizen ideology (6)	0.07	-0.11	-0.31	-0.19	0.00	1.00					
Corrections (7)	0.21	0.34	0.29	0.44	0.32	-0.11	1.00				
Civic engagement (8)	-0.10	-0.38	0.41	-0.66	-0.19	0.23	-0.36	1.00			
Gubernatorial power (9)	-0.06	-0.00	0.09	-0.20	-0.11	0.24	-0.28	0.22	1.00		
Marriage rate (10)	-0.07	0.22	0.03	-0.04	0.07	-0.13	0.08	-0.26	-0.14	1.00	
Metro. population (11)	0.28	0.49	0.32	0.24	0.36	0.31	0.40	-0.32	0.12	0.05	1.00

Table 6-3 MLE negative binomial regression coefficients (t values) from a series of random effects models of parole revocations, 1978-2007[a]

Variables[b]	(1) Baseline model	(2) Politics	(3) Sentencing	(4) All	(5) All + time	(6) Full model
Symbolic threats						
Economic threat	0.86*** (-5.64)	0.88*** (-5.14)	0.86*** (-5.48)	0.88*** (-4.94)	0.98 (-1.04)	0.97 (-0.88)
Economic threat^2	**1.05*** (4.18)	**1.06*** (4.45)	**1.05*** (4.18)	**1.06*** (4.44)	**1.06*** (5.03)	**1.05*** (4.38)
(ref=0-2% Black)	.	.	.	.	.	.
2-15% Black	**0.54*** (-8.39)	**0.64*** (-6.00)	**0.50*** (-8.74)	**0.61*** (-6.33)	**0.59*** (-7.16)	**0.66*** (-5.54)
Over 15% Black	**0.62*** (-5.54)	**0.81* (-2.36)	**0.57*** (-6.26)	**0.76** (-2.96)	**0.70*** (-4.72)	**0.74** (-3.26)
% Hispanic	0.99 (-1.73)	1.00 (0.27)	**0.99* (-2.35)	1.00 (-0.16)	**0.99* (-2.39)	1.00 (0.18)
Demographic variables						
Marriage rate	**1.01*** (6.79)	**1.01*** (7.94)	**1.01*** (6.75)	**1.02*** (7.95)	**1.02*** (8.42)	**1.02*** (9.66)
Metropolitan pop	**0.98*** (-13.32)	**0.98*** (-12.13)	**0.98*** (-12.97)	**0.98*** (-11.72)	**0.98*** (-12.18)	**0.98*** (-10.48)
% 18-24 yr-olds	**0.95*** (-4.11)	**0.97* (-2.51)	**0.94*** (-5.06)	**0.96*** (-3.51)	**1.15*** (6.79)	**1.17*** (7.52)
Politics						
Citizen ideology		1.00 (1.25)		1.00 (1.72)	1.00 (0.87)	1.00 (-0.51)
(ref=Dem. gov)		.		.	.	.
Rep. governor		1.00 (-0.06)		0.98 (-0.74)	0.99 (-0.62)	0.99 (-0.26)
Other governor		1.12 (0.99)		1.11 (0.93)	1.13 (1.06)	1.05 (0.49)
Civic engagement		**1.29*** (7.01)		**1.30*** (7.24)	**1.33*** (8.16)	**1.33*** (8.17)
Gubernatorial power		0.96 (-1.18)		0.97 (-0.93)	0.98 (-0.72)	1.03 (0.78)

Table 6-3 MLE negative binomial regression coefficients (t values) from a series of random effects models of parole revocations, 1978-2007a (Cond't)

Variables[b]	(1) Baseline model	(2) Politics	(3) Sentencing	(4) All	(5) All + time	(6) Full model
Sentencing structure						
(ref=No PBA[c])			.	.	.	.
Limited PBA			1.33^{***} (4.39)	1.36^{***} (4.76)	1.45^{***} (5.75)	1.33^{***} (4.38)
Full PBA			1.18^{***} (3.29)	1.20^{***} (3.61)	1.23^{***} (4.14)	1.22^{***} (4.03)
(ref=No guidelines)						
Voluntary guidelines			1.24^{***} (4.10)	1.24^{***} (4.10)	1.18^{**} (2.60)	1.20^{***} (3.59)
Presumptive guidelines			0.83^{**} (-2.78)	0.84^{**} (-2.69)	0.79^{***} (-3.72)	0.77^{***} (-3.76)
Time					1.05^{***} (10.12)	1.06^{***} (11.62)
Time^2					1.00^{***} (-9.54)	1.00^{***} (-11.09)
Crime						0.98 (-1.08)
Corrections						0.87^{***} (-6.13)
N	1294	1294	1294	1294	1294	1294
r	1.72	1.71	1.72	1.73	1.73	1.62
s	196.65	188.65	189.04	183.71	163.66	148.55
Wald chi2	498.83^{***}	566.77^{***}	561.07^{***}	641.07^{***}	691.70^{***}	780.92^{***}
Degrees of freedom	8.00	13.00	12.00	17.00	19.00	21.00
Likelihood ratio chi2	2358.20^{***}	2059.20^{***}	1576.93^{***}	1431.11^{***}	1391.17^{***}	1341.29^{***}

[a] Coefficients are reported as incidence rate ratios.

[b] All variables are lagged by one year.

[c] PBA: parole board authority

$^{*} p < 0.05,$ $^{**} p < 0.01,$ $^{***} p < 0.001$

Table 6-4 MLE negative binomial regression coefficients (t values) from a series of fixed effects models of parole revocations, 1978-2007a

Variables[b]	(1) Baseline model	(2) Politics	(3) Sentencing	(4) All	(5) All + time	(6) Full model
Symbolic threats						
Economic threat	0.85*** (-5.91)	0.87*** (-5.51)	0.85*** (-5.80)	0.87*** (-5.39)	0.97 (-1.04)	0.97 (-0.99)
Economic threat^2	**1.05***** (4.15)	**1.06***** (4.40)	**1.05***** (4.20)	**1.06***** (4.45)	**1.06***** (5.13)	**1.05***** (4.34)
(ref=0-2% Black)	.	.	.	.	.	.
2-15% Black	**0.50***** (-9.19)	**0.61***** (-6.80)	**0.47***** (-9.57)	**0.57***** (-7.14)	**0.58***** (-7.16)	**0.61***** (-6.47)
Over 15% Black	**0.59***** (-6.14)	**0.76**** (-3.02)	**0.53***** (-6.89)	**0.71***** (-3.68)	**0.64***** (-4.72)	**0.68***** (-4.14)
% Hispanic	0.99 (-1.90)	1.00 (-0.01)	**0.99*** (-2.54)	1.00 (-0.44)	**0.99*** (-2.39)	1.00 (-0.29)
Demographic variables						
Marriage rate	**1.01***** (6.73)	**1.02***** (7.83)	**1.01***** (6.67)	**1.02***** (7.81)	**1.02***** (8.42)	**1.02***** (9.57)
Metropolitan pop	0.98*** (-14.38)	**0.98***** (-13.15)	**0.98***** (-13.79)	**0.98***** (-12.51)	**0.98***** (-12.18)	**0.98***** (-11.18)
% 18-24 yr-olds	**0.95***** (-4.08)	**0.97*** (-2.38)	**0.94***** (-5.07)	**0.96***** (-3.42)	**1.15***** (6.79)	**1.17***** (7.71)
Politics						
Citizen ideology		1.00 (1.39)		1.00 (1.81)	1.00 (0.87)	1.00 (-0.47)
(ref=Democratic gov)		.		.	.	.
Republican governor		1.00 (0.13)		0.99 (-0.63)	0.99 (-0.62)	1.00 (-0.18)
Other governor		1.14 (1.18)		1.13 (1.09)	1.12 (1.06)	1.07 (0.62)
Civic engagement		**1.30***** (7.01)		**1.31***** (7.22)	**1.34***** (8.16)	**1.34***** (8.12)
Gubernatorial power		0.96 (-1.33)		0.97 (-1.09)	0.98 (-0.72)	1.02 (0.70)

Table 6-4 MLE negative binomial regression coefficients (t values) from a series of fixed effects models of parole revocations, 1978-2007[a] (Cond't)

Variables[b]	(1) Baseline model	(2) Politics	(3) Sentencing	(4) All	(5) All + time	(6) Full model
Sentencing structure						
(ref=No PBA[c])						
Limited PBA			**1.32***** (4.28)	**1.35***** (4.62)	**1.44***** (5.75)	**1.33***** (4.33)
Full PBA			**1.18**** (3.18)	**1.19***** (3.47)	**1.23***** (4.14)	**1.23***** (4.04)
(ref=No guidelines)						
Voluntary guidelines			**1.23***** (3.80)	**1.22***** (3.76)	**1.14**** (2.60)	**1.18**** (3.24)
Presumptive guid.			**0.82**** (-3.03)	**0.82**** (-2.93)	**0.77***** (-3.72)	**0.75***** (-4.10)
Time					**1.05***** (10.12)	**1.06***** (11.95)
Time^2					**1.00***** (-9.54)	**1.00***** (-11.09)
Crime						0.98 (-1.13)
Corrections						**0.87***** (-6.07)
N	1294	1294	1294	1294	1294	1294
Wald chi2	584.03***	665.14***	650.61***	743.15***	839.79***	893.54***
Degrees of freedom	8.00	13.00	12.00	17.00	19.00	21.00

[a] Coefficients are reported as incidence rate ratios.

[b] All variables are lagged by one year.

[c] PBA: parole board authority

* $p < 0.05$, ** $p < 0.01$, *** $p < 0.001$

The analysis of the sentencing covariates yields unexpected results as well. Indeed it was hypothesized that as discretion becomes more limited parole revocations would increase. This does not appear to be the case since greater parole board authority (i.e., more discretion) is related to increases in parole revocations (coefficients significant at $p<0.001$). Compared to states with no sentencing guidelines, voluntary guidelines are associated with an increase in parole revocations also, while the effect of presumptive guidelines (which presumably provide the most constraints on judicial discretion) is negative. Finally, there does appear to be a negative relationship between the weight of a state's correctional system (measured by the corrections index) and parole revocations.

Estimating period-specific relationships

The previous analyses show that several variables have a strong impact on parole revocations. However, by estimating a single coefficient for the entire 1978 to 2007 period, these models assume that the strength of these relationships is constant and stable over time, which is unlikely to be the case; the factors that ignited the prison boom in the 1970s and 1980s are not the same as the factors that sustained its growth in the 1990s (Blumstein and Beck 1999, 2005; Pfaff 2009; Stemen 2005), which are themselves different from those that explain the recent decarceration trend. Similarly, while the states have experienced significant growth in parole revocation rates over the last 30 years, this growth has not been uniform over time, and it is doubtful that the determinants of parole revocations in the 1980s are the same as the determinants of parole revocations in the 2000s. In particular, it is likely that significant differences exist between the last decade and the first two decades of the period, which may be due to the impact of the recent economic crisis. To explore this possibility, the study is divided into three time periods (1978-1988, 1989-1998, 1999-2007) corresponding to three phases in the growth of parole revocation rates, and the full model is replicated for each time period. The results of these models, which appear in Table 6.5, provide evidence that the factors responsible for the initial increase in parole revocation rates are not the same as those that have sustained this trend.

Table 6-5 MLE negative binomial regression coefficients (t values) from a series of random effects models of parole revocations stratified by time period, 1978-2007[a]

Variables	(1) **1978-1988**	(2) **1989-1998**	(3) **1999-2007**
Symbolic threats			
Economic threat	**0.89**[*] (-2.27)	0.94 (-1.31)	1.05 (1.02)
(ref=0-2% Black)	.	.	.
2-15% Black	**0.55**[**] (-3.25)	0.90 (-0.66)	0.83 (-1.83)
Over 15% Black	0.71 (-1.68)	1.00 (-0.02)	0.86 (-1.03)
% Hispanic	1.02 (1.87)	0.99 (-0.73)	**1.01**[*] (1.97)
Demographic variables			
Marriage rate	**1.01**[***] (4.11)	**1.01**[**] (3.18)	**1.02**[***] (3.98)
Metropolitan pop	**0.99**[**] (-2.85)	**0.96**[***] (-8.94)	**0.99**[***] (-3.99)
% 18-24 yr-olds	**0.85**[***] (-5.05)	0.96 (-1.35)	**1.14**[***] (3.82)
Politics			
Citizen ideology	1.00 (-0.13)	1.00 (0.58)	1.00 (-0.93)
(ref=Democratic gov.)	.	.	.
Republican governor	**1.13**[**] (3.27)	1.03 (0.76)	1.00 (-0.03)
Other governor	0.97 (-0.04)	0.88 (-0.93)	1.05 (0.22)
Civic engagement	1.09 (1.34)	**1.27**[***] (3.99)	**1.26**[***] (4.86)
Gubernatorial power	1.09 (1.21)	0.99 (-0.15)	0.92 (-1.14)
Sentencing structure			
(ref=No PB authority)			
Limited PB authority	1.14 (0.41)	1.27 (1.85)	1.23 (1.63)
Full PB authority	0.97 (-0.21)	1.03 (0.36)	1.22 (1.86)
(ref=No guidelines)			
Voluntary guidelines	1.16 (1.57)	1.09 (0.92)	1.03 (0.23)
Presumptive guid.	**0.46**[***] (-5.77)	**1.34**[**] (2.66)	0.81 (-1.39)
Crime	**0.85**[***] (-3.32)	0.98 (-0.55)	0.97 (-0.47)
Corrections	1.14 (1.89)	1.04 (1.01)	0.99 (-0.19)
N	417	483	394
r	2.25	1.11	2.55
s	88.10	80.26	165.14
Wald chi2	268.45[***]	267.38[***]	112.81[***]
Degrees of freedom	18.00	18.00	18.00
Likelihood ratio chi2	347.98[***]	407.80[***]	513.18[***]

[a] Coefficients are reported as incidence rate ratios.

[b] All variables are lagged by one year.

[c] PB: parole board

[*] $p < 0.05$, [**] $p < 0.01$, [***] $p < 0.001$

Specifically, the models present inconsistent support for the principal symbolic threat arguments advanced in the criminology literature. Economic and racial threats, for example, have an important impact on revocation rates during the 1980s; the coefficients for these variables are statistically significant ($p<0.05$ and $p<0.01$, respectively).

However, they do not have the anticipated effect on parole revocation. As the first model shows, a one-unit/standard deviation increase in the threat presented by economically marginalized populations is associated with an 11 percent decrease in revocation rates. This effect diminishes in the 1990s, and the relationship reverses itself in the 2000s, when economic threat becomes positively related to parole revocations levels in the states. This coefficient is not statistically significant however. The negative relationship between racial threats and parole revocation rates carries through all three periods, but it is statistically significant only during the 1980s, when states where between 2 and 15 percent of the population is Black have 45 percent lower parole revocation rates compared to states with very small (0 to 2 percent) Black populations ($p<0.01$). In contrast, states with larger Hispanic populations have higher incarceration rates. Percentage Hispanic becomes negatively associated with imprisonment during the 1990s, but the coefficient fails to achieve statistical significance. The relationship becomes positive again and significant during the 2000s. Therefore the research hypothesis concerning the effect of percentage Hispanic is supported only in the third period.

Surprisingly, political culture factors do not appear to be significant drivers of parole revocations, regardless of the period. States with a more liberal citizenry have higher levels of parole revocations throughout the period, but the coefficient is very small and not statistically significant. The relationship between Republican governor and parole revocations, positive through the 1980-90s (but significant only in the 1980s), becomes negative in the 2000s, which supports the hypothesis that partisan differences in crime policy decrease or even disappear entirely over time as both parties compete to be seen as tough-on-crime in order to win elections.

For the most part, the results concerning sentencing factors are not statistically significant. Presumptive guidelines have a strong influence on parole revocations in the 1980s and 90s, but become non-significant in the 2000s. Initially they are associated with lower parole revocations rates: in the 1980s, presumptive guidelines states have 54% ($p<0.001$)

lower parole revocation rates than states with no sentencing guidelines. However in the 1990s they have 34 percent (p<0.01) higher levels of revocations. The effect becomes negative again during the last period, but this coefficient is not statistically significant. Just as they were in the general model discussed earlier, voluntary guidelines states are consistently associated with more parole revocations compared to states that have no guidelines in the period-specific models as well, but these coefficients fail to reach statistical significance. Greater parole board authority is associated with a decrease in parole revocations only in the 1980s; thereafter the relationship becomes positive. These coefficients are not statistically significant either however.

Contrary to what was predicted the effect of civic engagement is positive throughout the period, and this factor becomes a strong predictor of parole revocations beginning in the 1990s. The relationship between crime and parole revocations is negative in all periods, but it is strongest and significant only during the 1980s, when a one standard deviation increase in the crime index was associated with a 15 percent decrease in parole revocations.

To put it another way, the results show that, in the 1980s, parole revocations were driven by economic and racial threats, partisan politics, sentencing factors, and crime. However, with the exception of Republican governor, none of the coefficients' signs for these variables are in the expected direction. Instead, the results show that economic threats, percentage Black, crime, and structured sentencing had a moderating effect on parole revocations during this period. The picture changes in the 1990s; results for this period are all non-significant, with the exception of presumptive guidelines and civic engagement, both positively associated with parole revocation levels. The last model indicates that the major determinants of parole revocations over the last few years have been ethnic threats and civic engagement.

DISCUSSION AND WIDER IMPLICATIONS

Summary of main findings

The goal of this chapter was to examine whether several factors that have been shown to drive incarceration rates exert an influence on state parole revocations. In the absence of a theoretical framework from which to understand variations in parole revocation rates, major findings from the criminological literature on the prison boom were used to develop and test a series of hypotheses using thirty years of aggregate data on all fifty American states.

The main findings can be summarized as follows. Several factors that have been shown in previous research to have an influence on incarceration rates or other dimensions of criminal justice in the U.S. also have an impact on parole revocation rates. The results of the full model (Model 6, Table 6.3) show that economic and racial threats, citizen engagement, sentencing structure, and corrections spending are all significantly associated with variations in parole revocations. Moreover, these variables seem to influence parole revocation rates in much the same way that they do incarceration rates, though the results from the time-stratified models complicate the story somewhat. These models provide only a very rough framework to understand how the social, political, cultural and structural underpinnings of the contemporary use of punishment have changed over the last 30-40 years, but they strongly suggest that parole revocations are driven primarily by historically contingent dynamics.

Let us consider crime rates. The negative relationship between crime rates and parole revocations casts doubt on the argument that states use parole revocation as a means of increasing social control and addressing concerns over rising crime rates. Another noteworthy finding of this study — that the number of parole revocations decreases as the weight of a state's correctional system (as measured by its incarceration rate and the proportion of state resources devoted to corrections) increases — provides a possible explanation for this unexpected relationship. Indeed, although corrections spending increased dramatically in the 1980s and 1990s and became an ever bigger piece of state budget pies (Stucky et al. 2007), incarceration rates increased at a faster pace still, taxing law enforcement and correctional resources and leaving states struggling to figure out how to handle overflowing facilities. Faced with the choice between devoting limited resources to either reining in crime rates or cracking down on parole violations, it is possible that states opted to focus law enforcement resources on addressing new crimes rather than parole violations and using whatever scarce correctional resources were available to house "more dangerous" offenders as opposed to parole violators who failed to abide by the conditions of their release but did not commit new crimes.

Also puzzling are the findings for threat effects. According to the results, neither economic threat, nor percentage Hispanic (although it is positive, the coefficient for ethnic threat is not significant and virtually indistinguishable from zero), are significant factors in variation in parole revocation rates. However, there is strong evidence that racial threats are associated with lower levels of parole revocations. As discussed in Chapter 2, it is not unusual for studies to find that race affects criminal justice outcomes, but ethnicity does not. The two groups enjoy a different status in the U.S. racial and ethnic hierarchy, where "Blacks have long been perceived as so physically and culturally different from Whites to warrant a separate 'racial' category both in the public mind and the legal sphere" (Dixon 2006, 2184; see also Muhammad 2010) but Hispanics are perceived as culturally assimilated, and therefore less threatening than Blacks. The perception that this group constitutes a lesser "threat" could be compounded by the fact that, until recently, Hispanics represented a small minority of the US population. This situation is changing rapidly as this demographic is increasing in size and distribution across the states quickly. Perhaps the significant, positive relationship between percentage Hispanic and parole revocation rates in the first decade of the twenty-first century is evidence that Hispanics are being perceived as a greater threat than they used to be.

But while the results of this study provide some support for the contention that the size of minority populations matters, the fact that percentage Black has a *negative* impact on parole revocations seems to contradict the theoretical basis for the threat argument that criminal justice policies are used to contain social groups (in this case, minorities) perceived as threatening to established structures of power and that, therefore, punitive reactions are likely to increase with the size of minority populations. This clearly is not the case here. Neither do the results provide evidence of the inverted U-shaped relationship between minority populations and harsh punishments that some studies have reported (Kane 2003; Keen and Jacobs 2009; Yates and Fording 2005). Authors typically explain this non-linear relationship by suggesting that racial threat is tied to voting power, so that once the African-American demographic becomes a large enough voting segment it is able to influence lawmakers and weaken the policies that produce racial disparities in the criminal justice system. The results reported here indicate that the negative effect of percentage Black state population on parole revocations *decreases* as percentage Black increases over 15 percent. If the political weight of this demographic group is indeed a factor, the results suggest that increasing the proportion of the state population that is Black over a certain threshold yields diminishing marginal returns in parole revocation rates.

For all the speculation in the criminological literature about the influence of a state's political culture on criminal justice policies and state punitive reactions, political factors do not appear to be important drivers of parole revocations. The results show that neither citizen ideology, nor Republican governor, has much impact on frequency of parole revocations. There is a negative relationship between Republican governor and parole revocation levels, but this variable's coefficient is not statistically significant. This, in itself, is not all that surprising; multiple studies have failed to find a relationship between party of governor and several aspects of criminal justice, most likely because differences between Republican and Democratic governors have narrowed over the last forty years as both parties have been compelled to respond to public pressures to be "tough on crime" by backing strong crime control measures. The time-stratified models indicate that this might be the case, as Republican governors are associated with increases in parole revocation rates during the 1980s and 1990s, and a decrease in the 2000s. However, only in the 1980s does this coefficient reach statistical significance.

The findings regarding the influence of state governance are more interesting. Barker (2006) was the first to draw researchers' attention to the importance of this factor. She contends that in order to understand why American states use punishment and confinement differently, one must look to differences in the democratic process in particular, to structures of state governance and practices of civic engagement. The findings of her comparative study of the states of California, New York, and Washington indicated that widespread civic engagement tends to moderate states' use of harsh punishments, and that the centralization of political authority works to insulate the state from public demands and to lead to a differentiated use of punishment.

The results reported here do not support Barker's arguments. They show on the basis of a 50-state study that an increase in the centralization of political authority (as measured by the index of gubernatorial power) is associated with an increase in parole revocations. However, it is noteworthy that this relationship is not statistically significant. Civic engagement, on the other hand, is a significant factor with a strong, <u>positive</u> impact on parole revocations; a one standard deviation increase in civic engagement is associated with a 33 percent increase in parole revocation rates, constituting one of the largest coefficients in the model. The sign of this coefficient contradicts Barker's assertion about the moderating role of civic engagement on state's punitive practices, but it is somewhat difficult to know what to make of these findings. It is possible that Barker's sample of three cases is too small to draw accurate conclusions about the role of civic engagement, or that the effects of civic engagement are mediated by other factors, such as citizen political ideology. Nevertheless, in spite of these differences, the results suggest that Barker is correct in drawing our attention to the importance of exploring differences in state democratic processes and coming up with better models of the influence of state governance on criminal justice outcomes. Such work is empirically beyond the scope of the current study, but is likely necessary to fully understand states' differentiated use of penal sanctioning.

But one of the most significant findings from the initial models concerns the influence of a state's sentencing structure on parole revocations. Not only are the coefficients for these variables strongly significant, but they also indicate that these factors have a large impact (relative to other covariates in the model) on the dependent variable. Perhaps because attacks on the indeterminate system were accompanied by calls to impose harsher penalties, many have been concerned that sentencing reforms (such as sentencing guidelines, mandatory sentences, truth-in-sentencing laws, or the abolition of parole boards) have contributed to the "prison boom" by curtailing the authority of judges and parole boards to decide how long offenders should spend behind bars. By placing discretion in the hands of the legislature instead, critics argue, sentencing decisions are more likely to be dictated by public demands for harsh punishments, including stricter enforcement of parole conditions. But generally speaking, this study found the opposite to be true: less structure/more discretion (as measured by the degree of authority of the parole board and the type of sentencing guidelines implemented in a state) is actually associated with higher levels of parole revocations.

Although this study cannot provide a good explanation for this result, one could speculate that where they do have the authority, parole board members (whose primary responsibility it is to weigh offender dangerousness against the safety of the community) tend to adopt conservative revocation strategies to minimize the risk to the community and to avoid making headlines for failing to revoke a parolee who goes on to commit a heinous crime. This argument is consistent with studies that found that discretionary parole is associated with longer time served, even when controlling for offense seriousness, prior record, age, gender and crime type (Hughes, Wilson and Beck 2001; Stivers 2001). The time-stratified models also indicate that parole boards may have become more risk-averse over time, perhaps a reaction to being faulted for being overly lenient, or in response to the general move toward harsher punishment practices. This line of argument is supported by the finding that in the 1980s greater parole board authority is associated with lower parole revocation rates, but the relationship changes direction in subsequent decades. Overall, these results suggest that limiting enactments, in the form of sentencing guidelines or limits to parole boards' authority, may be a moderating force in states' use of confinement.

Wider implications

As the first attempt to build a theoretical framework for understanding the use of parole revocation as a sanction in the states, this project raises more questions than it answers in some regards. From a theoretical perspective, the findings are both consistent with, and divergent from, the general prison boom literature. On the one hand, results demonstrate the complex, historically contingent nature of penal policymaking and support the continuing utility of considering those factors identified in the literature as significant drivers of criminal punishment practices in late modern American society. On the other hand (and more importantly perhaps), this study suggests that the framework used to explain incarceration may not be adequate to identify the factors most salient to parole revocation. The analyses thus help us to identify three broad lines of inquiry that require further empirical investigation.

While it can safely be assumed that parole policies and practices are subjected to the same macro-level social, political, and economic pressures that have shaped and transformed the system as a whole, what the findings of this study point to is that it will also be important to explore more carefully the mechanisms linking macro-level determinants to parole revocations, including any dynamic and interactive effects associated with the broader patterns identified in this study. The impact of state governance, for instance, may be shaped by the interactive effects of state structures with social organizations, political parties and political institutions. Its effects, therefore, may be different in the presence of different actors. Also, better models of punishment are needed that effectively integrate regional differences because there is evidence that variations in penal policies and practices can only be understood in the context of regional social, political, economic and cultural conditions. Finally, future research on parole outcomes could benefit from improvements to research design and data quality. As the first step toward building a framework for understanding the use of parole revocation as a punitive sanction, this study used very general social-demographic variables; but data more specific to parole such as administrative characteristics of states' parole organizations, or parole policies as well as other types of data such as interviews with parolees and other actors (parole agents, parole board members) involved would generate more insight and allow for a richer analysis by highlighting issues of discretion and sanctioning that are difficult to capture through socio-demographic measures or quantitative analyses of official statistics alone. Studies of parole in general, and parole revocation in particular, could benefit from improvements to data quality as well. Scholars have neglected to pay sufficient attention to back-end sentencing — in particular, the profound changes in the way that the parole system was managed, how it responded to the same get-tough impulses affecting every other aspect of criminal justice policy, and the relationship between parole revocations and the growth of the prison system. This relative neglect is apparent in the limited range and poor quality of the data that are available, even from such official sources as the venerable Bureau of Justice Statistics.

This study also suggests a policy implication that flows from the findings regarding the effects of the sentencing structure variables. As explained earlier, the popular "hydraulic displacement of discretion" argument that reducing the exercise of discretion at any point in criminal case processing will translate into more discretion exercised at other decision points in the justice system has generated both cynicism towards the potential effectiveness of policies designed to reduce disparities in the treatment of suspects/offenders by legal agents, and concerns about the adverse effects of these policies. These policies have been said to dehumanize the sentencing process and increase commitment and incarceration rates. This study cannot speak to the former, but does provide some evidence that concerns about the latter may be unfounded. Indeed, the analyses presented here reveal that any displacement of discretion (through the implementation of structured sentencing and the limitation of parole boards' authority) from the judiciary to the legislature did not result in higher parole revocation rates. As a matter of fact, curbing judicial discretion seems to be associated with *lower* parole revocation rates. This finding suggests that we need to revisit the criticisms leveled against grid-based sentencing schemes because they may present a valuable opportunity to achieve meaningful long-term changes in punishment patterns.

Chapter 7

Conclusion

Forty years after the country embarked on a massive overhaul of its penal philosophy and practices, American penal sanctioning is now "fragmented, multidimensional, and often contradictory" (Barker 2009: 6) and scholars still struggle to understand the factors behind the substantial amount of variation found in the use of imprisonment among the fifty states. Therefore, the goal of this research monograph was to investigate differences in the scope of penal sanctioning in the American states, with a particular focus on examining variation in state incarceration rates and state parole revocation rates over a thirty-year period (1978-2007). In so doing, this project (which belongs in the tradition of macro-sociological research that uses shifts in penology, political economy, demography and policy to analyze the country's imprisonment binge) offers a window into the changing historical understanding of the philosophy, the form, and the function of punishment in the United States. In addition, the research presented here makes three distinct contributions to the literature. First, it expands the analytical time frame and broadens the scope of theoretical explanations. Second, it examines how the determinants of sentencing practices have changed over time. Finally, it develops a framework for analyzing variations in state parole revocation rates; it constitutes the only study to date to attempt to shed some light on this crucial, yet overlooked criminal justice steering mechanism.

Results confirm that penal sanctioning, both at the front end and at the back end of the correctional system, is "overdetermined" (Garland 1990, 2001); state variation in incarceration rates and parole revocation rates is explained by a variety of factors ranging from differences in crime and social, political, economic and cultural conditions, to criminal justice policies; these represent forces that "built upon one another to produce the flow of prisoners into custody" (Garland 1990: 6) and create the patchwork of punishment practices that we see today. States have responded to similar policy problems with idiosyncratic policy solutions shaped by local social, political, economic and cultural conditions. The end result is the broad variation in the use of imprisonment that we see today among the states. As anticipated at the outset, the findings reported here also demonstrate that the influence of these factors on penal sanctioning is not constant over time, and that the determinants of incarceration rates and parole revocation rates are historically contingent. These relationships must be examined within their historical context if we are to understand paths and patterns of carceral state development across the country.

But perhaps the most significant finding to emerge from this project is that, while both front-end sentencing (court sentences) and back-end sentencing (parole revocations) are affected by the same forces, the ways in which these factors influence back end sentencing appear to be unique to back end sentencing. It is beyond the scope of this study to explain why this is the case, but this finding demonstrates that unless we devote more research attention to this crucial but overlooked component of the criminal justice system our knowledge of penal sanctioning in the U.S. will remain incomplete and our analytical models flawed and misleading.

An important limitation of macro-sociological research is that it privileges macrosociological patterns over microsociological experiences, and structural changes over the everyday practices of situated actors, and therefore assumes that social phenomena such as mass incarceration are primarily the result of a "top down" process. While such an approach provides valuable insights into the size and growth of prison populations, it understates the significance of other, micro-level factors (organizational constraints, for example, or the actions of local decision-makers such as court actors, parole agents, and interest groups) that shape punishment practices from the "bottom up." This study's finding that civic engagement is one of the factors most consistently associated with changes in incarceration rates and parole revocation rates testifies to the importance of this factor, but the results are difficult to explain because democratic theory is theoretically and empirically underdeveloped in the criminal justice literature. Building better models of civic engagement and participatory democracy that distinguish between constructive citizen involvement that takes responsibility for public problems, and mass politics mobilized superficially around hot-button issues would not only help explain variations in the contemporary use of penal sanctioning in the states, but also suggest possible ways to harness citizen participation to address the country's penal overindulgence from the ground up.

Appendix

Appendix A Percentage change in state incarceration rates, 1970-1985 and 1986-2002

State	Percentage Change in Incarceration Rate, 1970-1985	Percentage Change in Incarceration Rate, 1986-2002
Alabama	143%	129%
Alaska	339%	38%
Arizona	245%	100%
Arkansas	132%	146%
California	107%	150%
Colorado	20%	303%
Connecticut	101%	219%
Delaware	746%	61%
Florida	82%	82%
Georgia	72%	120%
Hawaii	298%	130%
Idaho	172%	247%
Illinois	207%	109%
Indiana	111%	99%
Iowa	83%	153%
Kansas	112%	70%
Kentucky	41%	186%
Louisiana	173%	158%
Maine	84%	70%
Maryland	123%	52%
Massachusetts	130%	166%
Michigan	84%	156%
Minnesota	39%	152%

Appendix A Percentage change in state incarceration rates, 1970-1985 and 1986-2002 (Cond't)

State	Percentage Change in Incarceration Rate, 1970-1985	Percentage Change in Incarceration Rate, 1986-2002
Mississippi	187%	214%
Missouri	153%	173%
Montana	284%	165%
Nebraska	56%	111%
Nevada	220%	22%
New Hampshire	143%	182%
New Jersey	106%	116%
New Mexico	135%	115%
New York	200%	77%
North Carolina	66%	36%
North Dakota	158%	193%
Ohio	129%	105%
Oklahoma	73%	167%
Oregon	76%	107%
Pennsylvania	166%	173%
Rhode Island	144%	93%
South Carolina	148%	89%
South Dakota	153%	159%
Tennessee	73%	189%
Texas	60%	206%
Utah	84%	138%
Vermont	76%	161%
Virginia	87%	125%
Washington	89%	67%
West Virginia	49%	181%
Wisconsin	104%	246%
Wyoming	91%	135%

Source: Stemen (2005)

Appendix B Investigating the 1991 and 1993 "dips" in parole revocation rates

Parole revocations followed an upward trend throughout the period covered in this study. As the number of people incarcerated grew, so did the number of prisoners released on parole, and consequently the number of parolees being revoked for violating the conditions of their release. As Figure B1 indicates, generally speaking, parole revocations increased rapidly in the 1980s, and more slowly thereafter. However two anomalous "dips," in 1991 and 1993, require a closer look. In those two years, the total number of parole revocations and national level revocation rates plunged dramatically, only to rebound a year later approximately to their previous levels. Averaged state-level revocation rates (the dotted line in Figure B1) exhibit the same pattern, though to a much lesser extent. This suggests that states with large parolee populations (California, for instance) could be driving the changes in national level revocation rates.

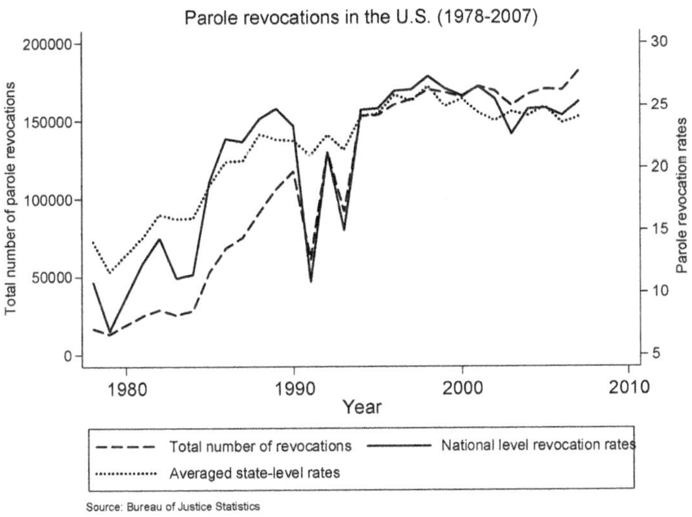

Figure B 1 Parole revocations in the U.S. (1978-2007)

To investigate this possibility, I examined scatterplots of state parole revocation rates between 1990 and 1995 (see Figures B2-B6). These graphs show that, while most states' revocation rates fluctuated somewhat during this period, for the most part they remained stable: there is little movement among states with low revocation rates (such as Wyoming), and states with revocation rates in the middle range (20 to 40 percent) such as Michigan, Colorado, Massachussetts or Kentucky. However, a few outlying cases show much greater variation from year to year. Alaska's parole revocation rate, for example, doubled between 1993 and 1994 (from 41.75 to 80 percent), and Florida's went from 1 percent to almost 30 percent. But Alaska's parole population of 412 in 1994 is much too small to be driving the changes seen on Figure B1.

A closer look at the data revealed that parole revocation data were missing for California in 1991 and 1993. In the early 1990s, the state counted about 80,000 parolees, about 50 percent of whom were getting revoked every year. This would suggest that the 1991 and 1993 "dips" are partly an artifact of these missing data. Although the data were vetted and published by the Bureau of Justice Statistics, they may not necessarily be complete or perfect. But it appears that greater-than-normal fluctuations in some state parole revocation rates (perhaps due to social, political, or economic developments unique to those states and those years) may also have contributed to altering parole revocation trends in the early 1990s.

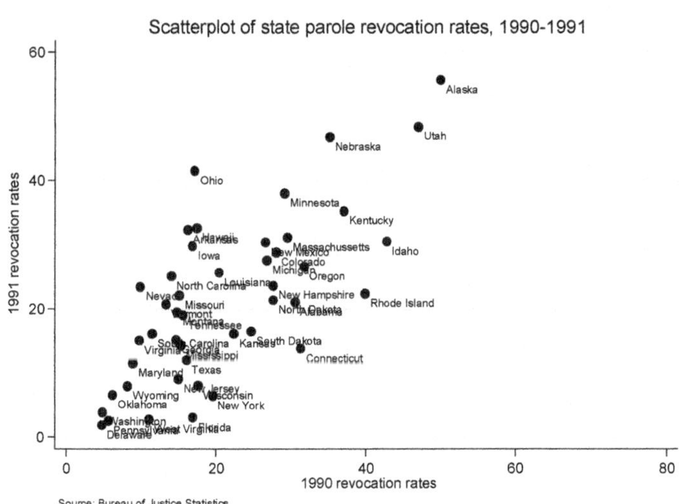

Figure B 2 Scatterplot of state parole revocation rates, 1990-1991

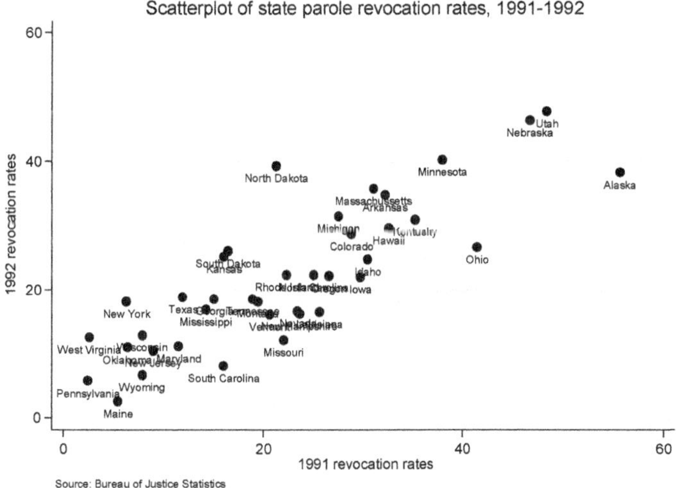

Figure B 3 Scatterplot of state parole revocation rates, 1991-1992

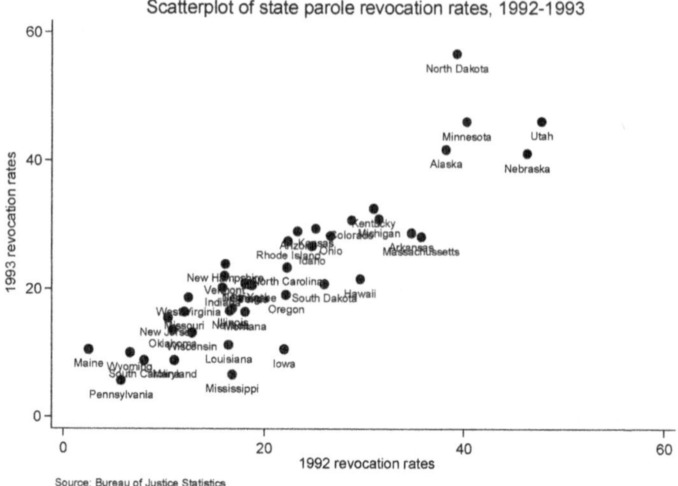

Figure B 4 Scatterplot of state parole revocation rates, 1992-1993

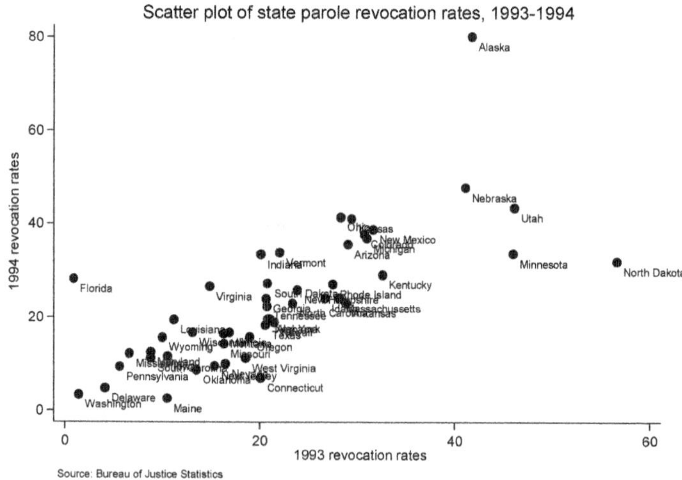

Figure B 5 Scatterplot of state parole revocation rates, 1993-1994

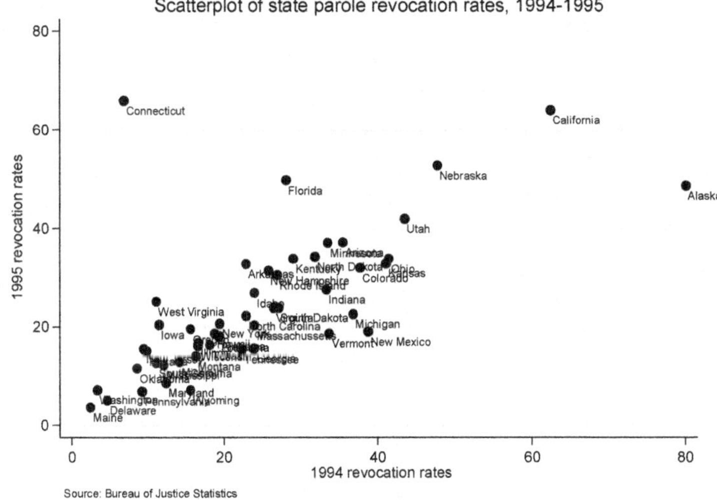

Figure B 6 Scatterplot of state parole revocation rates, 1994-1995

Appendix C Variables and their sources

Concept	Variable name	Variable description	Variable source
	rev_rt	Parole revocation rate—number of parolees returned to incarceration per 100 parolees under community supervision	Bureau of Justice Statistics: Correctional Populations series, Prisoners series, Probation and Parole in the US series, and Uniform Parole Reports, as well as unpublished data from the Annual Parole Survey series.
	incarc	Incarceration rate, per 100,000 residents	BJS, National Prisoner Statistics series
Crime, imprisonment, and releases	violcr_rt	Reported violent crimes per 100,000 resident population	FBI, Uniform Crime Reports [UCR], prepared by the National Archive of Criminal Justice Data
	propcr_rt	Reported property crimes per 100,000 resident population	FBI, Uniform Crime Reports [UCR], prepared by the National Archive of Criminal Justice Data
	incarc	Incarceration rate, per 100,000 residents	BJS, National Prisoner Statistics series

Appendix C Variables and their sources (Cond't)

Concept	Variable name	Variable description	Variable source
Symbolic threats	pct_black	Percentage population African-American	U.S. Census Bureau, Population Division; Centers for Disease Control and Prevention (CDC), National Center for Health Statistics (NCHS), Bridged-Race Population Estimates
	pct_hisp	Percentage population Hispanic (all races)	U.S. Census Bureau, Population Division; Centers for Disease Control and Prevention (CDC), National Center for Health Statistics (NCHS), Bridged-Race Population Estimates
	pct_empl	Percentage employed	Bureau of Labor Statistics, Employment status of the civilian non-institutional population, 1976 to 2009 annual averages, http://www.bls.gov/lau/rdscnp16.htm
	pct_pov	Percentage of the population living below the poverty level	US Census Bureau, Current Population Survey, Annual Social and Economic Supplements

Appendix C Variables and their sources (Cond't)

Concept	Variable name	Variable description	Variable source
Public opinion and partisan politics	cit_ideol	Citizen ideology index (0 = conservative, 100 = liberal)	Berry, Ringquist, Fording and Hanson, 1998; Fording, 2007, Most Recently Updated Citizen and Government Ideology Data, 1960-2008, http://rcfording.wordpress.com/state-ideology-data/
	gov_party	Party of Governor (0 = Democrat, 1 = Republican, 2 = other)	Carl Klarner, http://academic.udayton.edu/SPPQ-TPR/klarner_datapage.html
Centralization	gub_pwr	Index of Governors' Institutional Powers (5-point scale, 5 indicating greater power)	Beyle 2004, http://www.unc.edu/~beyle/gubnewpwr.html
Civic engagement	soc_cap voter_turn	State social capital score Voter turnout rates, 1980-2006	Putnam 2000 McDonald, United States Elections Project, http://elections.gmu.edu/voter_turnout.htm
Geography	region	Census regions, 4 categories: 1 = Northeast, 2 = Midwest, 3 = South, 4 = West	
Sentencing structure	par_abo	Parole board abolition (0 = no parole board, 1= parole board)	Stemen 2005
	pb_auth	Parole board authority (0 = none, 1 = very limited, 2 = limited, 3 = full)	Association of Paroling Authorities International, Annual Paroling Authorities Surveys
	pres_sent	Presumptive sentencing (0 = no, 1 = yes)	Stemen 2005
	sent_guid	Sentencing guidelines (0 = none, 1 = voluntary, 2 = presumptive)	Stemen 2005

Appendix C Variables and their sources (Cond't)

Concept	Variable name	Variable description	Variable source
Economy			*All data adjusted to 2007 constant dollars using the Consumer-Production Index*
	corr-sp	Corrections expenditures per capita	U.S. Census Bureau, Annual Survey of State Government Finances and Census of Governments
	educ_sp	Education expenditures per capita	U.S. Census Bureau, Annual Survey of State Government Finances and Census of Governments
	welf_sp	Welfare expenditures per capita	U.S. Census Bureau, Annual Survey of State Government Finances and Census of Governments
	tot_sp	Total expenditures per capita	U.S. Census Bureau, Annual Survey of State Government Finances and Census of Governments
	st_rev	State revenues per capita	U.S. Census Bureau, Annual Survey of State Government Finances and Census of Governments
	pers_inc	Personal income per capita	U.S. Census Bureau, Annual Survey of State Government Finances and Census of Governments

Appendix C Variables and their sources (Cond't)

Concept	Variable name	Variable description	Variable source
Prison overcrowding	crowd	Overcrowding (0 = no, 1 = yes)	BJS, various reports
Demographics	st_pop	State population	US Census Bureau, Population Division
	pct_metro	Percentage of the state's population living in metropolitan areas	Statistical Abstracts and Census Bureau, Population Division
	mar_rt	Number of marriages per 1,000 persons	Statistical Abstracts and U.S. National Center for Health Statistics, National Vital Statistics Reports
	youth	Percentage of the state population between the ages of 18 and 24	US Census Bureau, Population Division

Appendix D MLE negative binomial regression coefficients (t values) from a series of two-way fixed effects models of incarceration rates, 1978-2007[a]

Variables[b]	(1) Baseline model	(2) Politics	(3) Sentencing	(4) All	(5) All + time	(6) Full model
Economic threat	0.84*** (-11.42)	0.84*** (-12.16)	0.85*** (-11.42)	0.85*** (-12.47)	1.02 (1.84)	1.01 (1.23)
Economic threat^2	0.98*** (-3.71)	0.98** (-2.96)	0.98** (-2.89)	0.98** (-2.99)	1.00 (-0.59)	1.00 (0.31)
(ref=0-2% Black)						
2-15% Black	1.15*** (3.59)	1.13*** (3.78)	1.13*** (3.39)	1.13*** (3.78)	1.07*** (4.29)	1.09*** (5.00)
Over 15% Black	1.11* (2.23)	1.08 (1.82)	1.09* (1.96)	1.08 (1.82)	1.07* (2.55)	1.09*** (3.59)
% Hispanic	1.04*** (11.59)	1.05*** (11.78)	1.06*** (15.02)	1.06*** (15.33)	0.99*** (-3.30)	0.99 (-1.57)
Marriage rate	1.01*** (9.49)	1.01*** (8.72)	1.01*** (10.50)	1.01*** (8.97)	1.01*** (7.34)	1.01*** (7.04)
Metropolitan pop	1.01*** (6.26)	1.01*** (7.10)	1.01*** (7.21)	1.01*** (7.90)	1.00 (0.23)	1.00 (0.25)
% 18-24 yr-olds	0.87*** (-21.77)	0.87*** (-20.96)	0.87*** (-23.39)	0.88*** (-22.86)	1.02** (2.85)	1.01** (2.60)
Citizen ideology		1.00*** (-3.40)		1.00*** (-3.96)	1.00*** (-4.66)	1.00*** (-4.74)
(ref=Dem. Gov.)						
Republican governor		1.02* (2.36)		1.03** (3.09)	1.02*** (3.85)	1.02*** (3.67)
Other governor		0.97 (-0.95)		0.96 (-1.18)	0.98 (-0.99)	0.98 (-1.31)
Civic engagement		0.99 (-0.33)		1.00 (0.33)	1.00 (0.28)	1.00 (0.50)
Gubernatorial power		0.93*** (-4.33)		0.95*** (-3.60)	0.94*** (-4.72)	0.94*** (-5.34)
(ref=no PBA[c])						
Limited PBA			1.04 (1.19)	1.04 (1.37)	0.99 (-0.34)	0.99 (-0.42)
Full PBA			1.21*** (7.16)	1.22*** (7.83)	1.09*** (5.36)	1.10*** (5.84)
(ref=no guidelines)						
Voluntary guid.			1.21*** (7.60)	1.22*** (7.91)	1.04* (2.38)	1.03 (1.77)

Appendix D MLE negative binomial regression coefficients (t values) from a series of two-way fixed effects models of incarceration rates, 1978-2007[a] (Cond't)

Variables[b]	(1) Baseline model	(2) Politics	(3) Sentencing	(4) All	(5) All + time	(6) Full model
Presumptive guid.			1.16^{***} (5.53)	1.16^{***} (5.78)	0.94^{**} (-3.04)	0.95^{*} (-2.52)
Time					1.06^{***} (41.62)	1.06^{***} (41.14)
Time^2					1.00^{***} (-23.89)	1.00^{***} (-21.23)
Crime						1.04^{***} (4.52)
(ref=Alabama)						
Alaska	2.44^{*} (2.25)	3.24^{**} (3.00)	2.31^{*} (2.12)	2.79^{**} (2.63)	1.13 (0.27)	1.20 (0.40)
Arizona	0.29^{**} (-2.64)	0.26^{**} (-2.92)	0.32^{**} (-2.64)	0.33^{**} (-2.61)	1.01 (0.02)	1.02 (0.05)
Arkansas	2.42^{*} (2.21)	2.12 (1.90)	2.45^{*} (2.28)	2.12 (1.91)	2.45 (1.75)	2.88^{*} (2.13)
California	0.02^{***} (-8.85)	0.02^{***} (-8.10)	0.01^{***} (-9.83)	0.01^{***} (-9.30)	0.06^{***} (-6.03)	0.06^{***} (-6.04)
Colorado	0.13^{***} (-5.31)	0.17^{***} (-4.62)	0.22^{***} (-3.75)	0.29^{**} (-3.00)	0.19^{***} (-3.62)	0.18^{***} (-3.74)
Connecticut	0.33^{**} (-2.87)	0.48 (-1.85)	0.40^{*} (-2.33)	0.55 (-1.50)	0.45 (-1.71)	0.45 (-1.71)
Delaware	4.73^{***} (4.01)	4.44^{***} (3.84)	3.91^{***} (3.48)	3.65^{***} (3.33)	4.48^{***} (3.30)	4.97^{***} (3.54)
Florida	0.06^{***} (-6.51)	0.07^{***} (-6.05)	0.10^{***} (-5.45)	0.13^{***} (-4.98)	0.10^{***} (-5.06)	0.12^{***} (-4.59)
Georgia	0.63 (-1.17)	0.48 (-1.84)	1.42 (0.87)	1.25 (0.55)	0.34^{*} (-2.50)	0.28^{**} (-2.92)
Hawaii	0.57 (-1.43)	0.65 (-1.10)	0.58 (-1.39)	0.65 (-1.11)	1.84 (1.32)	1.70 (1.15)
Idaho	0.78 (-0.59)	1.11 (0.25)	0.84 (-0.41)	1.13 (0.29)	0.48 (-1.65)	0.52 (-1.37)
Illinois	0.35^{*} (-2.47)	0.48 (-1.72)	0.34^{**} (-2.62)	0.48 (-1.74)	0.42 (-1.79)	0.71 (-0.67)
Indiana	0.42^{*} (-2.18)	0.39^{*} (-2.39)	0.49 (-1.79)	0.44*2.10)	0.48 (-1.65)	0.45 (-1.76)
Iowa	0.75 (-0.62)	0.81 (-0.47)	0.77 (-0.58)	0.81 (-0.48)	0.70 (-0.79)	0.95 (-0.10)
Kansas	1.77 (1.43)	2.12 (1.87)	1.88 (1.55)	2.09 (1.83)	0.81 (-0.46)	0.69 (-0.81)

Appendix D MLE negative binomial regression coefficients (t values) from a series of two-way fixed effects models of incarceration rates, 1978-2007[a] (Cond't)

Variables[b]	(1) Baseline model	(2) Politics	(3) Sentencing	(4) All	(5) All + time	(6) Full model
Kentucky	0.43[*] (-2.11)	0.48 (-1.82)	0.40[*] (-2.31)	0.49 (-1.81)	0.29** (-2.59)	0.32[*] (-2.32)
Louisiana	0.42[*] (-2.21)	0.44[*] (-2.13)	0.59 (-1.38)	0.69 (-0.95)	2.13 (1.32)	1.42 (0.58)
Maine	1.50 (1.03)	1.92 (1.61)	2.18 (1.94)	2.70* (2.41)	0.26** (-3.18)	0.31** (-2.70)
Maryland	0.30** (-3.04)	0.30** (-3.00)	0.18*** (-4.35)	0.17*** (-4.40)	0.06*** (-6.45)	0.06*** (-6.38)
Massachusetts	0.13*** (-5.16)	0.12*** (-5.51)	0.13*** (-5.25)	0.12*** (-5.53)	0.07*** (-5.96)	0.08*** (-5.68)
Michigan	0.34** (-2.74)	0.39[*] (-2.42)	0.55 (-1.51)	0.52 (-1.62)	0.22*** (-3.49)	0.23*** (-3.35)
Minnesota	0.17*** (-4.58)	0.22*** (-3.84)	0.20*** (-4.06)	0.24*** (-3.59)	0.25** (-3.06)	0.27** (-2.89)
Mississippi	0.20*** (-4.11)	0.23*** (-3.74)	0.22*** (-3.73)	0.25*** (-3.44)	0.20*** (-3.33)	0.18*** (-3.53)
Missouri	0.87 (-0.32)	0.72 (-0.80)	0.43[*] (-2.13)	0.40[*] (2.26)	0.12*** (-4.41)	0.12*** (-4.24)
Montana	0.70 (-0.90)	0.87 (-0.36)	0.73 (-0.79)	0.85 (-0.41)	1.17 (0.35)	1.32 (0.60)
Nebraska	2.60[*] (2.25)	5.83*** (3.70)	3.88** (3.13)	7.66*** (4.42)	1.16 (0.32)	0.89 (-0.24)
Nevada	0.20*** (-3.70)	0.18*** (-3.88)	0.13*** (-4.77)	0.13*** (-4.91)	0.55 (-1.27)	0.46 (-1.59)
New Hampshire	0.79 (-0.60)	0.75 (-0.72)	0.80 (-0.55)	0.76 (-0.67)	0.49 (-1.59)	0.50 (-1.54)
New Jersey	0.07*** (-6.91)	0.09*** (-6.17)	0.05*** (-7.73)	0.06*** (-7.14)	0.08*** (-5.45)	0.09*** (-5.16)
New Mexico	0.56 (-1.30)	0.63 (-1.07)	0.45 (-1.69)	0.49 (-1.61)	4.40** (3.01)	3.26[*] (2.36)
New York	0.06*** (-7.37)	0.05*** (-7.40)	0.09*** (-6.06)	0.09*** (-6.08)	0.04*** (-7.50)	0.06*** (-5.86)
North Carolina	0.12*** (-5.48)	0.16*** (-4.61)	0.13*** (-5.16)	0.17*** (-4.43)	0.06*** (-6.53)	0.06*** (-6.64)
North Dakota	0.67 (-1.00)	0.82 (-0.50)	0.61 (-1.25)	0.69 (-0.93)	0.38[*] (-2.10)	0.44 (-1.77)
Ohio	0.17*** (-4.50)	0.19*** (-4.35)	0.17*** (-4.65)	0.18*** (-4.46)	0.15*** (-4.32)	0.18*** (-3.79)
Oklahoma	0.23*** (-3.75)	0.29** (-3.19)	0.27*** (-3.36)	0.32** (-2.91)	1.01 (0.02)	1.34 (0.61)

Appendix D MLE negative binomial regression coefficients (t values) from a series of two-way fixed effects models of incarceration rates, 1978-2007[a] (Cond't)

Variables[b]	(1) Baseline model	(2) Politics	(3) Sentencing	(4) All	(5) All + time	(6) Full model
Oregon	0.97 (-0.07)	1.58 (1.14)	1.12 (0.29)	1.62 (1.21)	1.49 (0.90)	1.36 (0.69)
Pennsylvania	0.07*** (-7.15)	0.08*** (-6.67)	0.08*** (-6.70)	0.09*** (-6.28)	0.13*** (-4.34)	0.17*** (-3.77)
Rhode Island	1.30 (0.68)	1.57 (1.17)	1.18 (0.42)	1.38 (0.81)	0.91 (-0.20)	0.96 (-0.10)
South Carolina	0.85 (-0.42)	1.27 (0.59)	3.12** (2.77)	3.01** (2.78)	0.32** (-2.58)	0.32** (-2.61)
South Dakota	1.41 (0.83)	1.78 (1.37)	0.88 (-0.31)	1.00 (-0.01)	0.85 (-0.35)	0.96 (-0.08)
Tennessee	0.52 (-1.68)	0.67 (-1.02)	0.35** (-2.68)	0.44* (-2.09)	0.12*** (-4.67)	0.13*** (-4.36)
Texas	0.02*** (-10.34)	0.01*** (-10.79)	0.02*** (-10.51)	0.01*** (-10.82)	0.01*** (-9.58)	0.01*** (-9.89)
Utah	0.35** (-2.68)	0.46* (-1.98)	0.40* (-2.33)	0.46* (-1.98)	1.46 (0.82)	1.55 (0.96)
Vermont	3.44** (2.97)	3.94* (3.28)	3.64** (3.13)	3.87** (3.28)	2.76* (2.18)	3.19* (2.42)
Virginia	1.79 (1.39)	1.83 (1.47)	1.58 (1.10)	1.77 (1.39)	0.63 (-1.03)	0.69 (-0.81)
Washington	0.30** (-3.11)	0.37* (-2.50)	0.38* (-2.41)	0.48 (-1.83)	0.35* (-2.30)	0.33* (-2.42)
West Virginia	0.63 (-1.13)	0.57 (-1.36)	0.57 (-1.40)	0.56 (-1.44)	0.10*** (-4.98)	0.12*** (-4.47)
Wisconsin	0.05*** (-8.12)	0.05*** (-7.94)	0.04*** (-8.78)	0.04*** (-8.77)	0.04*** (-7.26)	0.04*** (-7.21)
Wyoming	1.29 (0.64)	1.82 (1.47)	1.33 (0.71)	1.73 (1.36)	8.05*** (4.25)	9.18*** (4.46)
Observations	1448	1448	1448	1448	1448	1448
Wald chi2	9267.95	9496.99	10335.56	10753.36	29073.60	29061.54
Degrees of freedom	57.00	62.00	61.00	66.00	68.00	69.00

[a] Coefficients are reported as incidence rate ratios.

[b] All variables are lagged by one year.

[c] PBA: parole board authority

* $p < 0.05$, ** $p < 0.01$, *** $p < 0.001$

Appendix E MLE negative binomial regression coefficients (t values) from a series of two-way fixed effects models of parole revocation rates, 1978-2007[a]

Variables[b]	(1) Baseline model	(2) Politics	(3) Sentencing	(4) All	(5) All + time	(6) Full model
Economic threat	0.92*** (-3.63)	0.91*** (-3.99)	0.91*** (-3.98)	0.90*** (-4.22)	1.04 (1.33)	1.02 (0.83)
Economic threat^2	1.07*** (6.54)	1.07*** (6.68)	1.06*** (5.96)	1.07*** (6.12)	1.08*** (7.06)	1.08*** (7.18)
(ref=0-2% Black)						
2-15% Black	0.97 (-0.43)	0.99 (-0.22)	1.00 (-0.02)	1.01 (0.12)	1.00 (-0.02)	0.98 (-0.31)
Over 15% Black	1.19 (1.69)	1.20 (1.81)	1.24* (2.10)	1.25* (2.21)	1.24* (2.24)	1.24* (2.12)
% Hispanic	1.01 (1.29)	1.01 (0.85)	1.01 (1.79)	1.01 (1.41)	0.98* (-2.45)	0.99 (-1.55)
Marriage rate	1.01*** (4.55)	1.01*** (4.68)	1.01*** (4.62)	1.01*** (4.56)	1.01*** (3.72)	1.01*** (4.10)
Metropolitan pop	1.01 (-2.13)	1.00* (-2.17)	1.00* (-2.03)	1.00* (-1.96)	0.99*** (-3.34)	0.99*** (-3.57)
% 18-24 yr-olds	0.92*** (-7.92)	0.92*** (-7.70)	0.94*** (-6.40)	0.94*** (-6.28)	1.03 (1.85)	1.02 (1.60)
Citizen ideology		1.00 (0.97)		1.00 (0.95)	1.00 (0.45)	1.00 (0.25)
(ref=Dem. Gov.)						
Republican governor		1.02 (0.93)		1.01 (0.30)	1.01 (0.43)	1.01 (0.50)
Other governor		0.94 (-1.00)		0.93 (-1.12)	0.94 (-1.14)	0.93 (-1.29)
Civic engagement		1.30*** (1.01)		1.13 (1.02)	1.03 (0.82)	1.03 (0.97)
Gubernatorial power		1.03 (0.77)		0.97 (1.09)	1.09** (2.80)	1.10** (2.90)
(ref=no PBA[c])						
Limited PBA			1.12 (1.95)	1.12 (1.95)	1.19** (3.15)	1.18** (2.86)
Full PBA			1.16** (3.05)	1.16** (3.02)	1.18*** (3.88)	1.19*** (3.93)
(ref=no guidelines)						

Appendix E MLE negative binomial regression coefficients (t values) from a series of two-way fixed effects models of parole revocation rates, 1978-2007[a] (Cond't)

Variables[b]	(1) Baseline model	(2) Politics	(3) Sentencing	(4) All	(5) All + time	(6) Full model
Voluntary guid.			1.31^{***} (4.89)	1.30^{***} (4.89)	1.22^{***} (4.00)	1.22^{***} (3.93)
Presumptive guid.			0.99 (-0.08)	1.00 (-0.04)	0.92 (-1.27)	0.92 (-1.28)
Time					1.04^{***} (9.61)	1.04^{***} (9.22)
Time^2					1.00^{***} (-7.53)	1.00^{***} (-7.01)
Crime						1.02 (0.94)
Corrections						0.97 (-1.45)
(ref=Alabama)	.	.	.	.	.	.
Alaska	21.41^{***} (6.82)	20.24^{***} (6.68)	16.05^{***} (6.16)	15.57^{***} (6.09)	20.15^{***} (6.57)	19.38^{***} (6.47)
Arizona	4.94^{***} (3.81)	5.24^{***} (3.95)	3.19^{**} (2.73)	3.40^{**} (2.87)	6.33^{***} (4.24)	5.90^{***} (4.03)
Arkansas	1.95 (1.70)	1.90 (1.62)	1.87 (1.59)	1.82 (1.51)	2.28^{*} (2.07)	2.28^{*} (2.08)
California	0.96 (-0.07)	1.20 (0.33)	0.76 (-0.50)	0.85 (-0.29)	3.43^{*} (2.47)	2.87^{*} (2.04)
Colorado	23.02^{***} (7.62)	24.67^{***} (7.73)	22.73^{***} (7.53)	23.17^{***} (7.53)	63.89^{***} (9.27)	59.76^{***} (8.98)
Connecticut	4.14^{***} (3.47)	3.96^{***} (3.33)	4.15^{***} (3.47)	4.08^{***} (3.40)	7.83^{***} (4.75)	7.72^{***} (4.72)
Delaware	10.48^{***} (4.50)	9.77^{***} (4.35)	11.48^{***} (4.51)	11.04^{***} (4.43)	12.53^{***} (4.73)	12.69^{***} (4.75)
Florida	0.34^{**} (-2.73)	0.35^{**} (-2.65)	0.29^{**} (-3.12)	0.30^{**} (-3.06)	0.57 (-1.39)	0.53 (-1.54)
Georgia	0.98 (-0.05)	1.00 (-0.00)	1.01 (0.02)	1.00 (0.01)	1.28 (0.61)	1.29 (0.63)
Hawaii	6.68^{***} (4.64)	6.20^{***} (4.40)	6.45^{***} (4.56)	6.28^{***} (4.46)	8.05^{***} (5.01)	7.74^{***} (4.91)
Idaho	14.16^{***} (6.31)	14.47^{***} (6.34)	14.14^{***} (6.31)	14.73^{***} (6.39)	14.14^{***} (6.24)	13.38^{***} (6.08)
Illinois	0.48 (-1.80)	0.46 (-1.88)	0.55 (-1.44)	0.54 (-1.46)	0.83 (-0.42)	0.75 (-0.65)
Indiana	2.00 (1.64)	1.94 (1.57)	1.78 (1.36)	1.75 (1.32)	2.42^{*} (2.07)	2.40^{*} (2.04)
Iowa	7.16^{***} (4.70)	6.75^{***} (4.52)	7.48^{***} (4.79)	7.35^{***} (4.74)	7.98^{***} (4.90)	7.44^{***} (4.69)

Appendix E MLE negative binomial regression coefficients (t values) from a series of two-way fixed effects models of parole revocation rates, 1978-2007[a] (Cond't)

Variables[b]	(1) Baseline model	(2) Politics	(3) Sentencing	(4) All	(5) All + time	(6) Full model
Kansas	2.01 (1.75)	1.96 (1.68)	1.68 (1.27)	1.69 (1.27)	2.32[*] (2.02)	2.26 (1.95)
Kentucky	2.69[*] (2.47)	2.61[*] (2.39)	2.64[*] (2.41)	2.61[*] (2.38)	4.39[***] (3.64)	4.48[***] (3.68)
Louisiana	0.63 (-1.21)	0.63 (-1.19)	0.52 (-1.69)	0.52 (-1.69)	0. (-2.01)	0.49 (-1.82)
Maine	23.31[***] (5.84)	22.68[***] (5.74)	28.90[***] (6.19)	28.69[***] (6.13)	25.68[***] (6.14)	24.56[***] (5.96)
Maryland	3.68[**] (3.16)	3.35[**] (2.89)	2.44[*] (2.12)	2.31[*] (1.97)	2.83[*] (2.45)	2.88[*] (2.49)
Massachusetts	1.31 (0.69)	1.23 (0.51)	1.33 (0.72)	1.26 (0.57)	2.26[*] (1.96)	2.19 (1.87)
Michigan	3.35[**] (2.99)	3.18[**] (2.85)	4.81[***] (3.83)	4.72[***] (3.76)	5.70[***] (4.21)	5.94[***] (4.31)
Minnesota	27.53[***] (7.94)	29.93[***] (7.90)	34.20[***] (8.36)	37.89[***] (8.37)	66.21[***] (9.19)	63.19[***] (9.07)
Mississippi	0.93 (-0.17)	0.90 (-0.26)	1.45 (0.91)	1.44 (0.88)	1.74 (1.32)	1.56 (1.06)
Missouri	5.88[***] (4.30)	5.83[***] (4.25)	7.29[***] (4.79)	7.41[***] (4.81)	5.43[***] (4.00)	5.50[***] (4.04)
Montana	25.53[***] (7.41)	24.83[***] (7.30)	26.78[***] (7.49)	26.56[***] (7.43)	62.70[***] (8.29)	53.40[***] (7.88)
Nebraska	81.96[***] (10.09)	83.68[***] (9.96)	74.85[***] (9.96)	78.93[***] (9.93)	82.74[***] (10.02)	76.27[***] (9.77)
Nevada	4.48[**] (3.04)	4.42[**] (3.02)	4.58[**] (3.15)	4.53[**] (3.11)	10.17[***] (4.51)	9.62[***] (4.42)
New Hampshire	23.21[***] (6.84)	24.55[***] (6.88)	22.13[***] (6.76)	22.75[***] (6.79)	40.30[***] (7.92)	39.16[***] (7.82)
New Jersey	0.39[*] (-2.34)	0.39[*] (-2.35)	0.29[**] (-3.04)	0.29[**] (-3.04)	0.53 (-1.49)	0.50 (-1.63)
New Mexico	13.85[***] (5.24)	15.84[***] (5.54)	10.14[***] (4.62)	11.07[***] (4.78)	31.56[***] (6.53)	26.20[***] (5.92)
New York	0.88 (-0.31)	0.84 (-0.42)	0.87 (-0.35)	0.86 (-0.37)	1.57 (1.09)	1.50 (0.97)
North Carolina	1.13 (0.30)	1.13 (0.31)	1.31 (0.69)	1.31 (0.67)	1.73 (1.39)	1.68 (1.30)
North Dakota	40.80[***] (8.84)	39.90[***] (8.66)	40.15[***] (8.81)	39.50[***] (8.67)	54.50[***] (8.82)	52.77[***] (8.60)
Ohio	1.01 (0.02)	0.92 (-0.21)	0.78 (-0.60)	0.76 (-0.68)	0.79 (-0.58)	0.81 (-0.50)
Oklahoma	8.24[***] (4.99)	8.06[***] (4.91)	9.29[***] (5.25)	9.21[***] (5.20)	10.85[***] (5.52)	11.26[***] (5.60)

Appendix E MLE negative binomial regression coefficients (t values) from a series of two-way fixed effects models of parole revocation rates, 1978-2007[a] (Cond't)

Variables[b]	(1) Baseline model	(2) Politics	(3) Sentencing	(4) All	(5) All + time	(6) Full model
Oregon	1.19 (0.43)	1.24 (0.53)	1.59 (1.09)	1.61 (1.11)	2.18 (1.79)	2.14 (1.74)
Pennsylvania	0.22*** (-3.87)	0.20*** (-4.01)	0.22*** (-3.74)	0.22*** (-3.79)	0.28** (-3.17)	0.28** (-3.15)
Rhode Island	189.02*** (10.73)	190.40*** (10.54)	136.41*** (9.99)	129.09*** (9.76)	147.46*** (10.55)	149.35*** (10.52)
South Carolina	6.06*** (4.49)	5.46*** (4.15)	6.67*** (4.62)	6.36*** (4.44)	4.78*** (3.75)	4.70*** (3.65)
South Dakota	26.77*** (7.45)	25.84*** (7.30)	24.46*** (7.16)	24.85*** (7.13)	28.87*** (7.35)	26.11*** (7.01)
Tennessee	1.97 (1.72)	1.89 (1.61)	2.01 (1.76)	1.95 (1.69)	2.17 (1.95)	2.19* (1.96)
Texas	0.22** (-3.05)	0.23** (-3.01)	0.19*** (-3.39)	0.21** (-3.28)	0.59 (-1.05)	0.58 (-1.04)
Utah	27.65*** (8.03)	28.45*** (7.93)	48.80*** (8.91)	53.26*** (8.95)	65.46*** (8.80)	61.57*** (8.60)
Vermont	8.31*** (5.09)	7.81*** (4.87)	8.89*** (5.22)	8.46*** (5.04)	9.19*** (5.22)	8.66*** (5.00)
Virginia	1.76 (1.33)	1.72 (1.28)	1.49 (0.92)	1.47 (0.89)	2.24 (1.87)	2.32 (1.95)
Washington	0.65 (-0.99)	0.63 (-1.06)	0.79 (-0.54)	0.77 (-0.60)	1.26 (0.50)	1.18 (0.36)
West Virginia	3.79** (3.21)	3.52** (3.02)	4.11*** (3.39)	3.91** (3.25)	3.28** (2.83)	3.25** (2.78)
Wisconsin	5.00*** (3.86)	4.57*** (3.60)	4.05** (3.24)	3.90** (3.10)	7.23*** (4.57)	6.98*** (4.43)
Wyoming	24.33*** (7.18)	24.28*** (7.13)	25.28*** (7.23)	26.22*** (7.29)	54.47*** (8.17)	48.42*** (7.86)
Observations	1294	1294	1294	1294	1294	1294
chi2	1570.01	1581.25	1660.95	1667.26	1959.51	1970.97
Degrees of freedom	57.00	61.00	61.00	64.00	68.00	70.00

[a] Coefficients are reported as incidence rate ratios.

[b] All variables are lagged by one year.

[c] PBA: parole board authority

* $p < 0.05$, ** $p < 0.01$, *** $p < 0.001$

References

Adamson, Christopher. 1984. "Toward a Marxian Penology: Captive Criminal Populations as Economic Threats and Resources." *Social Problems* 31(4): 435-458.

Albonetti, Celesta A. 1991. "An Integration of Theories to Explain Judicial Discretion," *Social Problems* 38:247-66.

Alexander, Michelle. 2010. *The New Jim Crow: Mass Incarceration in the Age of Colorblindness.* New York: New Press.

Allen, Francis. 1981. *The Decline of the Rehabilitative Ideal.* New Haven, CT: Yale University Press.

Alschuler, Alan W. 1991. "The Failure of Sentencing Guidelines: A Plea for Less Aggregation." *University of Chicago Law Review* 58: 901-944.

Andrews, Day, and James Bonta. 1998. *The Psychology of Criminal Conduct* (2nd ed.). Cincinnati, OH: Anderson.

Association of Paroling Authorities, International. 2005. *Paroling Authorities Survey.* Available at http://www.apaintl.org/resources/surveys.html

Bales, William D., Gerry G. Gaes, Thomas G. Blumberg, and Kerensa N. Pate. 2010. "An Assessment of the Development and Outcomes of Determinate Sentencing in Florida," *Justice Research and Policy*, 12(1): 41-71.

Barker, Vanessa. 2006. "The Politics of Punishing: Building a State Governance Theory of American Imprisonment Variation." *Punishment and Society* 8(1): 5-32.

------. 2009. *The Politics of Imprisonment: How the Democratic Process Shapes the Way America Punishes Offenders.* New York: Oxford University Press.

Barron, David N. 1992. "The Analysis of Count Data: Overdispersion and Autocorrelation." *Sociological Methodology* 22: 179-220.

Barth, Fredrik. 1969. *Ethnic Groups and Boundaries.* Prospect, IL: Waveland Press.

Beck, Allen J. and Darrell K. Gilliard. 1995. *Prisoners in 1994.* Washington, D.C.: U.S. Department of Justice, Bureau of Justice Statistics.

Beckett, Katherine. 1997. *Making Crime Pay: Law and Order in Contemporary American Politics.* New York: Oxford University Press.

Beckett, Katherine and Theodore Sasson. 2000. *The Politics of Injustice: Crime and Punishment in America.* Thousand Oaks, CA: Pine Forge Press.

Behrens, Angela, Christopher Uggen, and Jeffrey Manza. 2003. "Ballot Manipulation and the 'Menace of Negro Domination': Racial Threat and Felon Disenfranchisement in the United States, 1850-2002." *American Journal of Sociology* 109: 559-605.

Beckett, Katherine and Bruce Western. 2001. "Governing Social Marginality: Welfare, Incarceration, and the Transformation of State Policy." *Punishment and Society* 3: 43-59.

Berry, William D., Evan J. Ringquist, Richard C. Fording and Russell L. Hanson. 1998. "Measuring Citizen and Government Ideology in the American States, 1960-93." *American Journal of Political Science* 42(1): 327-348. Updated Citizen and Government Ideology Data, 1960-2008, is available at http://rcfording.wordpress.com/state-ideology-data/

Berry, William D., Richard C. Fording, Evan J. Ringquist, Russell L. Hanson and Carl Klarner. 2010. "Measuring Citizen and Government Ideology in the American States: A Re-appraisal." *State Politics and Policy Quarterly* 10: 117-35.

Bevir, Mark and R. A. W. Rhodes. 2010. *The State as Cultural Practice.* New York, NY: Oxford University Press.

Beyle, Thad. 2004. "Gubernatorial Power: The Institutional Power Ratings for the 50 Governors in the United States." Accessed at http://www.unc.edu/~beyle/gubnewpwr.html in June 2014.

Binder, Amy. 2007. "For Love and Money: Organizations' Creative Responses to Multiple Environmental Logics." *Theory and Society* 36: 547-571.

Blalock, Hubert M. 1967. *Toward a Theory of Minority-Group Relations.* New York: Wiley.

Blumer, Herbert. 1980. "Mead and Blumer: The Convergent Methodological Perspectives of Social Behaviorism and Symbolic Interactionism." *American Sociological Review,* 45(3): 409-419.

Blumstein, Alfred and Allen J. Beck. 2005. "Reentry as a Transient State Between Liberty and Recommitment." Pp. 50-79 in *Prisoner Reentry and Crime in America,* edited by J. Travis and C. Visher. Cambridge, MA: Cambridge University Press.

Blumstein, Alfred and Allen J. Beck. 1999. "Population Growth in U. S. Prisons, 1980-1996." *Crime and Justice* 26 (Prisons): 17-61.

Bobo, Lawrence. 1999. "Prejudice as Group Position: Microfoundations of a Sociological Approach to Racism and Race Relations." *Journal of Social Issues* 55: 445-72.

Bobo, Lawrence and Vincent L. Hutchings. 1996. "Perceptions of Racial Group Competition: Extending Blumer's Theory of Group Position to a Multiracial Social Context." *American Sociological Review* 61(6): 951.

Bollen, Kenneth A. and Patrick J. Curran. 2006. *Latent Curve Models: A Structural Equation Perspective.* Hoboken, NJ: John Wiley and Sons.

Bonczar, Thomas P. 2003. *Prevalence of Imprisonment in the U.S. Population, 1974-2001.* Washington, D.C · Bureau of Justice Statistics.

Bonilla-Silva, Eduardo. 1997. "Rethinking Racism: Toward a Structural Interpretation." *American Sociological Review* 62(3): 465-480.

Borg, Marian J. 1997. "The Southern Subculture of Punitiveness? Regional Variation in Support for Capital Punishment." *Journal of Research in Crime and Delinquency* 34(1): 25-45.

Bottomley, Keith A. 1990. "Parole in Transition: A Comparative Study of Origins, Developments, and Prospects for the 1990s." Pp. 319-374 in *Crime and Justice: A Review of Research*, v.12, edited by Michael Tonry and Norval Morris. Chicago: University of Chicago Press.

Bottoms, Anthony. 1995. "The Philosophy and Politics of Punishment and Sentencing." Pp. 17–49 in *The Politics of Sentencing Reform*, ed. by C. Clarkson and R. Morgan. Oxford: Oxford University Press.

------.1983. "Neglected Features of Contemporary Penal Systems." Pp. 166-202 in *The Power to Punish*, edited by D. Garland and P. Young. London: Heinemann.

Bottoms, Anthony and Paul Wiles. 1995. "Crime and Insecurity in The City." Pp. 1-38 in *Changes in Society, Crime and Justice in Europe*, edited by C. Fijnaut, J. Goethals, T. Peters and L. Walgrave. The Hague: Kluwer.

Bourdieu, Pierre. 1987. "The Force of Law: Toward a Sociology of the Juridical Field." *Hastings Law Review* 38:805-53.

------ and Loic Wacquant. 1992. *An Invitation to Reflexive Sociology.* Chicago: University of Chicago Press.

Bowers, D. A. and J. L. Waltman. 1993. "Do More Conservative States Impose Harsher Felony Sentences? An Exploratory Analysis of 32 States." *Criminal Justice Review* 18: 61-70.

Brace, Paul, Kevin Arceneaux, Martin Johnson, and Stacy Ulbig. 2004. "Does State Political Ideology Change Over Time?" *Political Research Quarterly* 57(4): 529-40.

Bridges, George S. and Robert D. Crutchfield. 1988. "Law, Social Standing and Racial Disparities in Imprisonment." *Social Forces* 66(3): 699-724.

Britt, Chester L. 2000. "Social Context and Racial Disparities in Punishment Decisions." *Justice Quarterly* 17(4): 707-732.

Brown, M. Craig and Barbara D. Warner. 1995. "The Political Threat of Immigrant Groups and Police Aggressiveness in 1900." Pp. 82-98 in *Ethnicity, Race, and Crime*, edited by D.F. Hawkins. Albany, NY: State University of New York Press.

Burke, Peggy. 2004. *Parole Violations Revisited: A Handbook on Strengthening Parole Practices for Public Safety and Successful Transition to the Community.* Silver Spring, MD: Center for Effective Public Policy.

------. 2003. *A Handbook for New Parole Board Members: Part of a Resource Kit for New Parole Board Members.* Silver Spring, MD: Center for Effective Public Policy.

Bursik, Robert J. and Harold G. Grasmick. 1993. *Neighborhoods and Crime.* New York: Lexington.

Caldeira, Gregory A. 1983. "Elections and the Politics of Crime: Budgetary Choices and Priorities in America." Pp. 238-52 in *The Political Science of Criminal Justice*, edited by S. Nagel, E. Fairchild and A. Champagne. Springfield, IL: Charles C. Thomas.

Caldeira, Gregory A. and Andrew T. Cowart. 1980. "Budgets, Institutions, and Change: Criminal Justice Policy in America." *American Journal of Political Science* 24: 413-38.

Cameron, A. Colin and Pravin K. Trivedi. 1986. "Econometric Models Based on Count Data: Comparisons and Applications of Some Estimators and Tests." *Journal of Applied Econometrics* 1: 29-54.

Campbell, Michael C. 2011. "Politics, Prisons, and Law Enforcement: An Examination of the Emergence of 'Law and Order' Politics in Texas." *Law and Society Review* 45(3): 631-66.

------. 2012. "Ornery Alligators and Soap on a Rope: Texas Prosecutors and Punishment Reform in the Lone Star State." *Theoretical Criminology* 16(3): 289-311.

Campbell, Michael C. and Heather Schoenfeld. 2013. "The Transformation of America's Penal Order: A Historicized Political Sociology of Punishment." *American Journal of Sociology* 118(5): 1375-1423.

Campbell, Nancy M. 2008. *Comprehensive Framework for Paroling Authorities in an Era of Evidence-Based Practices.* Washington, D.C.: National Institute of Corrections.

Campbell, Robin. 2003. *Dollars and Sentences.* New York: Vera Institute of Justice. Retrieved February 21, 2011 http://www.vera.org/content/dollars-and-sentences-legislators-views-prisons-punishment-and-budget-crisis.

Cappell, Charles L. and Gresham Sykes. 1991. "Prison Commitments, Crime, and Unemployment: A Theoretical and Empirical Specification for the United States, 1933-1985." *Journal of Quantitative Criminology* 7(2): 155-199.

Carroll, John S. 1978. "Causal Attributions in Expert Parole Decisions," *Journal of Personality and Social Psychology* 36: 1501-11.

Casper, Jonathan and David Brereton. 1984. "Evaluating Criminal Justice Reforms." *Law and Society Review* 18: 121-144.

Chambliss, William J. 1994. "Policing the Ghetto Underclass: The Politics of Law and Law Enforcement." *Social Problems* 41(2): 177-194.

Chambliss, William J. and R. Seidman. 1982. *Law, Order and Power.* Reading, MA: Addison-Wesley.

Chiricos, Theodore G. and Miriam A. Delone. 1992. "Labor Surplus and Punishment: A Review and Assessment of Theory and Evidence." *Social Problems* 39(4): 421-446.

Chiricos, Theodore G., Kelly Welch, and Marc G. Gertz. 2004. "Racial Typification of Crime and Support for Punitive Measures." *Criminology* 42: 359-389.

Clear, Todd R. 2007. *Imprisoning Communities: How Mass Incarceration Makes Disadvantaged Neighborhoods Worse.* New York: Oxford University Press.

Clear, Todd R. and James Austin. 2009. "Reducing Mass Incarceration: Implications of the Iron Law of Prison Populations." *Harvard Law and Policy Review* 3: 307-324.

Cohen, Jacqueline and José A. Canelo-Cacho. 1994. "Incarceration and Violent Crime: 1965-1988." Pp. 296-388 in *Understanding and Preventing Violence*, edited by A.J. Reiss and J.A. Roth. Washington, DC: National Academy Press.

Colvin, Mark. 1990. "Labor Markets, Industrial Monopolization, Welfare, and Imprisonment: Evidence from a Cross-Section of U.S. Counties." *The Sociological Quarterly* 31(3): 441-457.

Cook, Kimberly M. 1995. *Punitiveness and Public Opinion on Abortion and Capital Punishment in the United States.* Doctoral dissertation, The University of New Hampshire, 1994. *Dissertation Abstracts International*, 55, 3650.

Cullen, Francis T., Bonnie S. Fisher, and Brandon K. Applegate. 2000. "Public Opinion about Punishment and Corrections." *Crime and Justice: A review of Research* 27: 1-79.

Cullen, Francis T., and Paul Gendreau. 1989. "The Effectiveness of Correctional Treatment: Reconsidering the 'Nothing Works' Debate." In *The American Prison: Issues in Research and Policy,* edited by L. Goodstein and D. L. MacKenzie. New York: Plenum Press.

Cunningham, David. 2012. "Mobilizing Ethnic Competition." *Theory and Society* 41: 505-512.

Cunningham, David and Benjamin Phillips. 2007. "Contexts for Mobilization: Spatial Settings and Klan Presence in North Carolina, 1964-1966." *American Journal of Sociology* 113: 781-814.

Davey, Joseph D. 1998. *The Politics of Prison Expansion: Winning Elections by Waging War on Crime.* Westport, CT: Praeger.

Davis, Angela. 2003. *Are Prisons Obsolete?* New York: Seven Stories.

De Giorgi, Alessandro. 2006. *Re-thinking the Political Economy of Punishment: Perspectives on Post-Fordism and Penal Politics.* Burlington, VT: Ashgate.

Dixon, Travis L. 2006a. "Psychological Reactions to Crime News Portrayals of Black Criminals: Understanding the Moderating Roles of Prior News Viewing and Stereotype Endorsement." *Communication Monographs* 73: 162–187.

------. 2006b. "Schemas as Average Conceptions: Skin Tone, Television News Exposure, and Culpability Judgments." *Journalism and Mass Communication Quarterly* 83:131–149.

Donziger, Steven R. 1996. *The Real War on Crime.* New York: Harper Collins.

Edsall, Thomas B. and Mary D. Edsall. 1991. *Chain Reaction: The Impact of Race, Rights, and Taxes on American Politics.* New York: Norton.

Enns, Peter K. 2014. "The Public's Increasing Punitiveness and Its Influence on Mass Incarceration in the United States." *American Journal of Political Science.* Retrieved July 2014 from http://dx.doi.org/10.1111/ajps.12098.

Erikson, Robert S., Gerald C. Wright Jr. and John P. McIver. 1989. "Political Parties, Public Opinion, and State Policy in the United States." *The American Political Science Review* 83(3): 729-750.

Fagan, Jeffrey, Valerie West and Jan Holland. 2003. "Reciprocal Effects of Crime and Incarceration in New York Neighborhoods." *Fordham Urban Law Journal* 30: 1551-1602.

Feeley, Malcolm and Jonathan Simon. 1992. "The New Penology: Notes on the Emerging Strategy of Corrections and Its Implications." *Criminology* 30(4): 449-474.

Felson, Marcus and Lawrence Cohen. 1980. "Human Ecology and Crime: A Routine Activities Approach." *Human Ecology* 8(4): 389-406.

Finckenauer, James O. 1978. "Crime As A National Political Issue: 1964-76." *Crime & Delinquency* 24(1): 13-27.

Foucault, Michel. 1995. *Discipline and Punish: The Birth of the Prison.* 2nd ed. New York: Vintage Books.

Fox, Cybelle and Thomas A. Guglielmo. 2012. "Defining America's Racial Boundaries: Blacks, Mexicans, and European Immigrants, 1890-1945." *American Journal of Sociology* 118: 327-379.

Frase, Richard S. 1995. "State Sentencing Guidelines: Still Going Strong." *Judicature* 78: 173-179.

------. 1991. "Defendant Amenability to Treatment or Probation as a Basis for Departure under the Minnesota and Federal Sentencing Guidelines." *Federal Sentencing Reporter* 3: 328-333.

Frey, William H. 2002. "Three Americas: The Rising Significance of Regions." *Journal of the American Planning Association* 68(4): 349-355.

Frost, Natasha A. 2008. "The Mismeasure of Punishment: Alternative Measures of Punitiveness and Their (Substantial) Consequences." *Criminology & Penology* 10(3): 277-300.

Gardner, William, Edward P. Mulvey, and Esther C. Shaw. 1995. "Regression Analyses of Counts and Rates: Poisson, Overdispersed Poisson, and Negative Binomial." *Psychological Bulletin* 118: 392–405.

Garland, David. 2001. *The Culture of Control: Crime and Social Order in Contemporary Society.* Chicago: University of Chicago Press.

------. 1996. "The Limits of the Sovereign State: Strategies of Crime Control in Contemporary Society." *British Journal of Criminology* 36(4): 445-471.

------. 1990. *Punishment and Modern Society: A Study in Social Theory.* Chicago: University of Chicago Press.

------. 1985. *Punishment and Welfare: A History of Penal Strategies.* Brookfield, VT: Gower.

Gephart, Martha A. 1997. "Neighborhoods and Communities as Contexts for Development." Pp. 1-43 in *Neighborhood Poverty Volume 1: Context and Consequences for Children*, edited by J. Brooks-Gunn, G.J. Duncan and J.L. Aber. New York, NY: Russell Sage Foundation.

Gilmore, Ruth W. 2007. *Golden Gulag: Prison, Surplus, Crisis, and Opposition in Globalizing California*. Berkeley: University of California Press.

Glaze, Lauren and Seri Palla. 2005. *Probation and Parole in the United States, 2004*. Washington, D.C.: Bureau of Justice Statistics.

Gottschalk, Marie. 2006. *The Prison and the Gallows: The Politics of Mass Incarceration in America*. Cambridge: Cambridge University Press.

Gouldner, Alvin W. 1954. *Patterns of Industrial Bureaucracy*. Glencoe, Ill.: Free Press.

Grattet, Ryken, Joan Peterselia, Jeffrey Lin and Marlene Beckman. 2009. "Parole Violations and Revocation in California: Analysis and Suggestions for Action." *Federal Probation* 73(1): 2-11.

Greenberg, David. 1999. "Punishment, Division of Labor, and Social Solidarity." Pp. 283-361 in *The Criminology of Criminal Law: Advances in Criminological Theory*, edited by W.S. Laufer and F. Adler. New Brunswick, NJ: Transaction.

------. 1977. "The Dynamics of Oscillatory Punishment Processes." *Journal of Criminal Law and Criminology* 68: 643-651.

Greenberg, David and Valerie West. 2001. "State Prison Populations and Their Growth, 1971-1991." *Criminology* 39: 615-653.

Griset, Pamala L. 1991. *Determinate Sentencing: The Promise and The Reality of Retributive Justice*. Albany, NY: State University of New York Press.

Gullickson, Aaron. 2010. "Racial Boundary Formation at the Dawn of Jim Crow." *American Journal of Sociology* 116:187-231.

Hallett, Tim and Marc J. Ventresca. 2006. "Inhabited Institutions: Social Interactions and Organizational Forms in Gouldner's *Patterns of Industrial Bureaucracy*." *Theory and Society* 35(2): 213-236.

Hamilton, Claire. 2014. "Reconceptualizing Penality: Towards a Multidimensional Measure of Punitiveness." *British Journal of Criminology* 54: 321-343.

Harcourt, Bernard E. 2006. "From the Asylum to the Prison: Rethinking the Incarceration Revolution," *Texas Law Review*, 84: 1751-86.

------. 2007. *Against Prediction: Profiling, Policing, and Punishing in an Actuarial Age*. Chicago: University of Chicago Press.

Harding, David. 2003. "Counterfactual Models of Neighborhood Effects: The Effect of Neighborhood Poverty on Dropping Out and Teenage Pregnancy." *American Journal of Sociology* 109:676-720.

Harrison, Paige M. and Allen J. Beck. 2003. *Prisoners in 2002.* Washington, D.C.: Bureau of Justice Statistics.

Hawkins, Darnell F. 1987. "Beyond Anomalies: Rethinking the Conflict Perspective on Race and Criminal Punishment." *Social Forces* 65(3): 719-745.

Hawkins, Darnell F. and Kenneth A. Hardy. 1989. "Black-White Imprisonment Rates: A State-by-State Analysis." *Social Justice* 16(4): 75-94.

Haydu, Jeffrey. 1998. "Making Use of the Past: Time Periods as Cases to Compare and Sequences of Problem Solving." *American Journal of Sociology* 104(2): 339-371.

Hernes, Gudmund. 1976. "Structural Change in Social Process." *American Journal of Sociology* 82: 513-547.

Hicks Alexander M. 1994. "Introduction to Pooling." In *The Comparative Political Economy of the Welfare State,* Thomas Janoski and Alexander Hicks (eds), Cambridge, MA: Cambridge University Press.

Hirsch, Paul and Michael Lounsbury. 1997. "Ending the Family Quarrel: Toward a Reconciliation of 'Old' and 'New' Institutionalism." *American Behavioral Scientist* 40:406-418.

Hsiao, Cheng. 1986. *Analysis of Panel Data.* New York: Cambridge University Press.

Huber, Evelyne, Charles Ragin and John D. Stephens. 1993. "Social Democracy, Christian Democracy, Constitutional Structure, and the Welfare State." *The American Journal of Sociology* 99(3): 711-749.

Huber, Gregory A. and Sanford C. Gordon. 2004. "Accountability and Coercion: Is Justice Blind when It Runs for Office?" *American Journal of Political Science* 48(2): 247-263.

Huebner, Beth M. and Timothy S. Bynum. 2008. "The Role of Race and Ethnicity in Parole Decisions." *Criminology* 46(4): 907-938.

------. 2006. "An Analysis of Parole Decision Making Using a Sample of Sex Offenders: A Focal Concerns Perspective," *Criminology* 44: 961-91.

Huff, C. Ronald and John M. Stahura. 2006. "Police Employment and Suburban Crime." *Criminology* 17(4): 461-470.

Hughes, Timothy A., Doris J. Wilson and Allen J. Beck. 2001. *Trends in State Parole, 1990-2000.* Special Report. Bureau of Justice Statistics. Washington, D.C.: U.S. Department of Justice, Office of Justice Programs.

Ignatieff, Michael. 1978. *A Just Measure of Pain: The Penitentiary in the Industrial Revolution, 1750-1850.* London: Macmillan.

Immergut, Ellen M. 1992. *Health Politics: Interests and Institutions in Western Europe.* New York: Cambridge University Press.

Isaac, Larry W., and Larry J. Griffin. 1989. "Ahistoricism in Time-Series Analyses of Historical Process: Critique, Redirection, and Illustrations from U.S. Labor History." *American Sociological Review* 54: 873-890.

Jackson, Pamela I. and Leo Carroll. 1981. "Race and the War on Crime: The Socio-Political Determinants of Municipal Police Expenditures in 90 Non-Southern US Cities." *American Sociological Review* 46: 290-305.

Jacobs, David and Jason T. Carmichael. 2001. "The Politics of Punishment across Time and Space: A Pooled Time-Series Analysis of Imprisonment Rates." *Social Forces* 80(1): 61-89.

Jacobs, David, Jason T. Carmichael, and Stephanie L. Kent. 2005. "Vigilantism, Current Racial Threat, and Death Sentences." *American Sociological Review* 70: 656-677.

Jacobs, David and Ronald Helms. 1999. "Collective Outbursts, Politics, and Punitive Resources: Toward a Political Sociology of Spending on Social Control." *Social Forces* 77(4): 1497-1523.

Jacobs, David, Zhenchao Qian, Jason T. Carmichael, and Stephanie L. Kent. 2007. "Who Survives on Death Row? An Individual and Contextual Analysis." American Sociological Review 72(Aug.): 610-632.

Jacobson, Michael. 2006. "Revering the Punitive Turn: The Limits and Promise of Current Research." Criminology and Public Policy 5(2): 277-284.

Johnson, Brian D. 2005. "Contextual Disparities in Guidelines Departures: Courtroom Social Contexts, Guidelines Compliance, and Extralegal Disparities in Criminal Sentencing," *Criminology* 43: 761-96.

Johnson, Brian D., Jeffery T. Ulmer, and John H. Kramer. 2008. "The Social Context of Guidelines Circumvention: The Case of Federal District Courts," *Criminology* 46: 737-83.

Johnson, John and John DiNardo. 1997. *Econometrics Methods*, Fourth Edition. McGraw-Hill.

Jones, Bryan. 1999. "Bounded Rationality," *Annual Review of Political Science* 2: 297-321.

Kane, Robert J. 2003. "Social Control in the Metropolis: A Community-Level Examination of the Minority Group-Threat Hypothesis." Justice Quarterly 20 (2): 265-295.

Katznelson, Ira. 1997. "Reflections on History, Method, and Political Science." *Political Methodologist* 8: 11-14.

Kautt, Paula M. and Miriam A. Delone. 2006. "Sentencing Outcomes Under Competing but Coexisting Sentencing Interventions: Untying the Gordian Knot." *Criminal Justice Review* 31: 105-131.

Keen, Bradley and David Jacobs. 2009. "Racial Threat, Partisan Politics, and Racial Disparities in Prison Admissions: A Panel Analysis." *Criminology* 47(1): 209-238.

Kennedy, Peter. 2003. *A Guide to Econometrics*, fifth edition. Cambridge, MA: MIT Press.

King, Ryan D., Steven F. Messner, and Robert D. Baller. 2009. "Contemporary Hate Crimes, Law Enforcement, and the Legacy of Racial Violence." *American Sociological Review* 74: 291-315.

King, Ryan D. and Darren Wheelock. 2007. "Group Threat and Social Control: Race, Perceptions of Minorities and the Desire to Punish." *Social Forces* 85: 1255-80.

Klarner, Carl. 2003. "Measurement of Partisan Balance of State Government." *State Politics and Policy Quarterly* 3: 309-19.

Klarner, Carl, William Berry, Thomas Carsey, Malcolm Jewell, Richard Niemi, Lynda Powell, and James Snyder. State Legislative Election Returns (1967-2010). ICPSR34297-v1. Ann Arbor, MI: Inter-university Consortium for Political and Social Research [distributor], 2013-01-11. http://doi.org/10.3886/ICPSR34297.v1

Kramer, John. 1992. "The Evolution of Pennsylvania's Sentencing Guidelines." *Overcrowded Times* 3: 6-9.

Kramer, John H. and Jeffery T. Ulmer. 1996. "Sentencing Disparity and Departures from Guidelines." *Justice Quarterly* 13(1): 81.

Kubrin, Charis E. and Eric A. Stewart. 2006. "Predicting Who Reoffends: The Neglected Role of Neighborhood Context in Recidivism Studies." *Criminology* 44: 165-197.

Kutateladze, Besiki. 2009. *Is America Really So Punitive? Exploring a Continuum of U.S. State Criminal Justice Policies*. El Paso, TX: LFB Scholarly Publishing.

LaFree, Gary. 1998. *Losing Legitimacy: Street Crime and the Decline of Social Institutions in America*. Boulder, CO: Westview Press.

Land, Kenneth C., Patricia L. McCall, and Lawrence E. Cohen. 1990. "Structural Covariates of Homicide Rates: Are There Any Invariances Across Time and Social Space?" *American Journal of Sociology* 95(4): 922-963.

Langan, Patrick A. 1991. "America's Soaring Prison Population." *Science* 251(5001): 1568-1573.

Lassiter, Matthew D. 2006. *The Silent Majority: Suburban Politics in the Sunbelt South.* Princeton, N.J.: Princeton University Press.

Lessan, Gloria T. 1991. "Macro-Economic Determinants of Penal Policy: Estimating the Unemployment and Inflation Influences on Imprisonment Rate Changes in the United States, 1948-1985." *Crime, Law and Social Change* 16: 177-198.

Levitt, Steven D. 1996. "The Effect of Prison Population Size on Crime Rates: Evidence from Prison Overcrowding Litigation." *The Quarterly Journal of Economics* 111(2): 319-351.

Lin, Jeffrey, Ryken Grattet, and Joan Petersilia. 2010. "Back-end Sentencing and Reimprisonment: Individual,Organizational, and Community Predictors of Parole Sanctioning Decisions." *Criminology* 48(3): 759-795.

Lipsky, Michael. 1980. *Street-Level Bureaucracy.* New York: Russell Sage Foundation.

Lipson, Albert J. and Mark A. Peterson. 1980. *California Justice under Determinate Sentencing.* Santa Monica, CA: RAND.

Liska, Allen E., Joseph J. Lawrence and Michael Benson. 1981. "Perspectives on the Legal Order: The Capacity of Social Control." *American Journal of Sociology* 87: 412-426.

Listokin, Yair. 2003. "Does More Crime Mean More Prisoners? An Instrumental Variables Approach." *Journal of Law and Economics* 46(1): 181-206.

Long, J. Scott. 1997. *Regression Models for Categorical and Limited Dependent Variables.* Thousand Oaks, CA: Sage.

Lynch, James. 1993. "A Cross-National Comparison of the Length of Custodial Sentences for Serious Crimes." *Justice Quarterly* 10(4): 639-660.

Lynch, Mona. 2011."Mass incarceration, legal change and locale: Understanding and remediating American penal overindulgence." *Criminology & Public Policy*10: 671-698.

------. 2011. "Theorizing Punishment: Reflections on Wacquant's *Punishing the Poor.*" *Critical Sociology* 37(2): 237-244.

------. 2010. *Sunbelt Justice: Arizona and the Transformation of American Punishment.* Stanford, CA: Stanford University Press.

------. 2004. "Rehabilitation as Rhetoric: The Ideal of Reformation in Contemporary Parole Discourse and Practices." *Punishment and Society* 2(1): 40-65.

------. 1998. "Waste Managers? The New Penology, Crime Fighting, and Parole Agent Identity." *Law and Society Review* 32(4): 839-870.

Maguire, Kathleen and Ann L. Pastore. 2002. *Sourcebook of Criminal Justice Statistics.*

Manza, Jeff and Christopher Uggen. 2006. *Locked Out: Felon Disenfranchisement and American Democracy.* New York: Oxford University Press.

March, James, and Herbert A. Simon. 1958. *Organizations.* New York: Wiley.

Martinson, Robert. 1974. "What works? Questions and answers about prison reform." *The Public Interest* 35 (Spring): 22–54.

Marvell, Thomas B. 1995. "Sentencing Guidelines and Prison Population Growth." *Journal of Criminal Law and Criminology* 85: 696-709.

Marvell, Thomas B. and Carlisle E. Moody. 1996. "Determinate Sentencing and Abolishing Parole: The Long-Term Impacts on Prisons and Crime." *Criminology* 34(1): 107-128.

Marx, Karl, Friedrich Engels and Samuel Moore. 1955; [1955, c1952]. *Capital.* Oxford: Oxford University Press.

Matthews, Roger. 2005." The Myth of Punitiveness." *Theoretical Criminology* 9(2): 175-201.

Mauer, Marc and Ryan S. King. 2007. *Uneven Justice: State Rates of Incarceration by Race and Ethnicity.* Washington, D.C.: The Sentencing Project. Accessed June 2014 at http://www.sentencingproject.org/doc/publications/rd_stateratesofincbyraceandethnicity.pdf

McBride, Elizabeth C. 2009. "Policing Parole: The Constitutional Limits of Back-End Sentencing." *Stanford Law and Policy Review* 20(2): 597-621.

McCoy, Candace. 1984. "Determinate Sentencing, Plea Bargaining Bans, and Hydraulic Discretion in California." *The Justice System Journal* 9: 256-275.

McDonald, Michael P. 2012. "Presidential Voter Turnout Rates, 1948-2012." *United States Elections Project,* accessed in June 2014 at http://elections.gmu.edu/voter_turnout.htm.

McGirr, Lisa and American Council of Learned Societies. 2001. *Suburban Warriors: The Origins of The New American Right.* Princeton, N.J.: Princeton University Press.

McVeigh, Rory. 2009. *The Rise of the Ku Klux Klan: Right-Wing Movements and National Politics.* Minneapolis, MN: University of Minnesota Press.

McVeigh, Rory and David Cunningham. 2012. "Enduring Consequences of Right-Wing Extremism: Klan Mobilization and Homicides in Southern Counties." Social Forces 90: 843-62.

Miethe, Terance D. 1987. "Charging and Plea Bargaining Practices Under Determinate Sentencing: An Investigation of the Hydraulic Displacement of Discretion." *Journal of Criminal Law and Criminology* 78: 155-176.

Moehling, Carolyn and Anne Morrison Piehl. 2009. "Immigration, Crime, and Incarceration in Early Twentieth Century America." *Demography* 46: 739-63.

Morenoff, Jeffrey D., Robert J. Sampson and Stephen W. Raudenbush. 2001. "Neighborhood Inequality, Collective Efficacy, and the Spatial Dynamics of Urban Violence." *Criminology* 39: 517-559.

Morone, James A. 2003. *Hellfire Nation: The Politics of Sin in American History.* New Haven: Yale University Press.

Morris, Norval. 2002. *Maconochie's Gentlemen: The Story of Norfolk Island and the Roots of Modern Prison Reform.* New York: Oxford University Press.

Muhammad, Khalil G. 2010. *The Condemnation of Blackness: Race, Crime, and the Making of Modern Urban America.* Cambridge, Mass.: Harvard University Press.

Muller, Christopher. 2012. "Northward Migration and the Rise of Racial Disparity in American Incarceration, 1880-1950." *American Journal of Sociology* 118: 281-326.

Mundlak, Yair. 1978. "On the Pooling of Time Series and Cross Section Data." *Econometrica* 46(1): 69-85.

Myers, Martha A. and Susette M. Talarico. 1987. *The Social Contexts of Criminal Sentencing.* New York: Springer-Verlag.

Neal, Derek and Armin Rick. 2014. "The Prison Boom and the Lack of Black Progress After Smith and Welch." *National Bureau of Economic Research* Working Paper No. 20283, July 2014, JEL No. J01,J31,L14.

Neapolitan, Jerome L. 2001. "An Examination of Cross-National Variation in Punitiveness." *International Journal of Offender Therapy and Comparative Criminology* 45(6): 691-710.

Nicholson-Crotty, Sean. 2004. "The Impact of Sentencing Guidelines on State-Level Sanctions: An Analysis Over Time." *Crime and Delinquency,* 50(3): 395-411.

North Carolina Division of Adult Probation and Parole Revocation Task Force. 1995. *Impacting Probation/Parole Revocations: Final Report.* North Carolina Department of Corrections.

Oliver, Pamela E. 2008. "Repression and Crime Control: Why Social Movement Scholars Should Pay Attention to Mass Incarceration as a Form of Repression." *Mobilization* 13: 1-24.

Oliver, Pamela E. and James E. Yocom. "Explaining State Black Imprisonment Rates 1983-1999." Unpublished manuscript, presented at the American Sociological Association meeting August 2004.

Olzak, Susan and Suzanne Shanahan. 2014. "Prisoners and Paupers: The Impact of Group Threat on Incarceration in Nineteenth-Century U.S. Cities." *American Sociological Review* 79: 392-411.

O'Malley, Pat. 1992. "Risk, Power, and Crime Prevention." *Economy and Society* 21: 252-275.

Ouimet, Marc and Pierre Tremblay. 1996. "A Normative Theory of the Relationship between Crime Rates and Imprisonment Rates: An Analysis of the Penal Behavior of the US States from 1972 to 1992." *Journal of Research on Crime and Delinquency* 33: 109-125.

Page, Joshua. 2012. "Punishment and the Penal Field." Pp. 152-166 in *SAGE Handbook on Punishment and Society*, ed. by Jonathan Simon and Richard Sparks. London: Sage.

Pager, Devah. 2007. *MARKED: Race, Crime, and Finding Work in an Era of Mass Incarceration.* Chicago: University of Chicago Press.

Palermo, George B., Maurice B. Smith, and Frank J. Liska. 1991. "Jails Versus Mental Hospitals: A Social Dilemma," *International Journal of Offender Therapy and Comparative Criminology,* 35(2): 97-106.

Petersilia, Joan. 1999. "Parole and Prisoner Reentry in the United States." *Crime and Justice* 26 (Prisons): 479-529.

------. 2003. *When Prisoners Come Home: Parole and Prisoner Reentry.* New York: Oxford University Press.

Pfaff, John F. March 2007. *The Growth of Prisons: Toward a Second Generation Approach.* Fordham University School of Law.

------. 2008. "The Empirics of Prison Growth: A Critical Review and Path Forward." *Journal of Criminal Law and Criminology* 98(2): 547-619.

------. 2009. "The Myths and Realities of Correctional Severity: Evidence from the National Corrections Reporting Program on Sentencing Practices." *Fordham University School of Law Research Paper no. 1338365.* Retrieved February 10, 2011 SSRN: http://ssrn.com/abstract=1338365.

Pindyck, Robert S. and Daniel L. Rubinfeld. 1991. *Econometric Models and Economic Forecasts.* McGraw-Hill.

Piven, Frances F. and Richard A. Cloward. 1971. *Regulating the Poor: the Functions of Public Welfare.* New York: Pantheon Books.

Podesta, Federico. 2002. "Recent Developments in Quantitative Comparative Methodology: The Case of Pooled Time Series Cross-Section Analysis." Retrieved June 2014: http://www.unibs.it/sites/default/files/ricerca/allegati/1233pode202.pdf

Pontell, Henry N. 1984. *A Capacity to Punish: The Ecology of Crime and Punishment.* Bloomington: Indiana University Press.

Pontell, Henry N., and Wayne N. Welsh. 1994. "Incarceration as a Deviant Form of Social Control: Jail Overcrowding in California." *Crime and Delinquency* 40: 18–36.

Putnam, Robert D. 2000. *Bowling Alone: The Collapse and Revival of American Community.* New York: Simon and Schuster.

Rabe-Hesketh, S. and Anders Skrondal. 2008. *Multilevel and Longitudinal Modeling Using Stata.* College Station, Tex.: Stata Press.

Raphael, Steven. 2009. "The Impact of Incarceration on the Employment Outcomes of Former Inmates: Policy Options for Fostering Self-Sufficiency and an Assessment of the Cost-Effectiveness of Current Corrections Policy." Pp185-226 in *Making the Work-Based Safety Net Work Better: Forward Looking Policies to Help Low-Income Families,* edited by C. J. Heinrich and K. Sholz. New York: Russell Sage Foundation.

Raphael, Steven and Michael Stoll. 2013. "Assessing the Contribution of the Deinstitutionalization of the Mentally Ill to Growth in the U.S. Incarceration Rate," *Journal of Legal Studies* 42(1): 187-222.

------. 2009. "Why Are So Many Americans in Prison?" Pp. 27-72 in *Do Prisons Make Us Safer? The Benefits and Costs of the Prison Boom,* edited by S. Raphael and M. Stoll. New York: Russell Sage.

Steven Raphael, Michael A. Stoll, Mark Duggan and Anne Morrison Piehl. 2004. "The Effect of Prison Releases on Regional Crime Rates." *Brookings-Wharton Papers on Urban Affairs* 2004: 207-255.

Rathke, Stephen C. 1982. "Plea Negotiating Under the Sentencing Guidelines." *Hamline Law Review* 5: 271-291.

Reichman, Nancy. 1986. "Managing Crime Risks: Toward an Insurance Based Model of Social Control." *Research in Law, Deviance, and Social Control* 8:151-72.

Reitz, Kevin R. 2001. "The Disassembly and Reassembly of U.S. Sentencing Practices." Pp. 222-258 in *Sentencing and Sanctions in Western Countries*, edited by R. Frase and M. Tonry. New York: Oxford University Press.

Reitz, Kevin and Curtis Reitz. 1993. The American Bar Association's New Sentencing Standards, Federal Sentencing Reporter 6(3):169.

Rosich, Katherine J. 2007. "Race, Ethnicity, and the Criminal Justice System." Washington, D.C.: American Sociological Association (http://asanet.org).

Rothman, David J. 1983. "Sentencing Reforms in Historical Perspective." *Crime and Delinquency* 29: 631-647.

------. 1990. *The Discovery of the Asylum: Social Order and Disorder in the New Republic.* Boston: Little, Brown.

------. 1980. *Conscience and Convenience: the Asylum and its Alternatives in Progressive America.* Boston: Little, Brown.

Ruggles-Brise, Sir, Evelyn. 1921. *English Prison System.* London: MacMillan.

Rusche, Georg and Otto Kirschheimer. 1968. *Punishment and Social Structure.* New York: Russell and Russell.

Sabol, William J. 2002. *Influences of Truth-in-Sentencing Reforms on Changes in States' Sentencing Practices and Prison Populations.* Washington, D.C.: U.S. Department of Justice, National Institute of Justice.

Sampson, Robert J., Jeffrey D. Morenoff and Thomas Gannon-Rowley. 2002. "Assessing "Neighborhood Effects": Social Processes and New Directions in Research." *Annual Review of Sociology* 28: 443-478.

Sampson, Robert J., Jeffrey D. Morenoff and Stephen Raudenbush W. 2005. "Social Anatomy of Racial and Ethnic Disparities in Violence." *American Journal of Public Health* 95: 224-232.

Sampson, Robert J., Stephen W. Raudenbush and Felton Earls. 1997. "Neighborhoods and Violent Crime: A Multilevel Study of Collective Efficacy." *Science* 227: 918-924.

Savelsberg, Joachim. 1994. "Knowledge, Domination, and Criminal Punishment." *American Journal of Sociology* 99: 911-943.

Scheingold, Stuart A. 1991. *The Politics of Street Crime: Criminal Process and Cultural Obsession.* Philadelphia: Temple University Press.

------. 1998. "Constructing the New Political Criminology: Power, Authority, and the Post-Liberal State." *Law and Social Inquiry* 23(4): 857-895.

Schlesinger, Traci. 2011. "The Failure of Race Neutral Policies: How Mandatory Terms and Sentencing Enhancements Contribute to Mass Racialized Incarceration." *Crime and Delinquency*: 56-81.

Schneider, Saundra K., and William G. Jacoby. 2006. "Citizen Influences on State Policy Priorities: The Interplay of Public Opinion and Interest

Groups." Pp. 183-208 in *Public Opinion in State Politics*, ed. Jeff Cohen. Stanford University Press.

Schoenfeld, Heather. 2011. "Crime or Insecurity: Who Is The 'State'? And What Is It 'Responding' To?" *Punishment and Society* 13(4):473-479.

------. 2014. "The Delayed Emergence of Penal Modernism in Florida." Punishment and Society 16(3): 258-284.

Scully, Maureen. 1997. "Stealth Legitimacy: Employee Activism and Corporate Response During the Diffusion of Domestic Partner Benefits." Paper presented at the Academy of Management Meetings, Boston MA, August.

Seiter, Richard P. 2002. "Prisoner Reentry and the Role of Parole Officers." *Federal Probation* 66: 50-54.

Seiter, Richard P. and Angela D. West. 2003. "Supervision Styles in Probation and Parole: An Analysis of Activities." *Journal of Offender Rehabilitation* 38(2): 57-75.

Sharkansky, Iva. 1969. "The Utility of Elazar's Political Culture: A Research Note." *Polity* 2: 66-83.

Shaver, Kelly G. 1975. *An Introduction to Attribution Process*. Cambridge, MA: Winthrop.

Shaw, Clifford and Henry D. McKay. 1942. *Juvenile Delinquency and Urban Areas: A Study of Rates of Delinquency in Relation to Differential Characteristics of Local Communities in American Cities*. Chicago: University of Chicago Press.

Simon, Herbert A. 1991. "Bounded Rationality and Organizational Learning." *Organizational Science* 2: 125-34.

Simon, Jonathan. 1993. *Poor Discipline: Parole and the Social Control of the Underclass, 1890-1990*. Chicago: University of Chicago.

------. 2007. *Governing Through Crime: How the War on Crime Transformed American Democracy and Created a Culture of Fear*. New York: Oxford University Press.

Singer, Judith D. and John B. Willett. 2003. *Applied Longitudinal Data Analysis: Modeling Change and Event Occurrence*. New York: Oxford University Press.

Skocpol, Theda and Edwin Amenta. 1986. "States and Social Policies." *Annual Review of Sociology* 12: 131-157.

Smith, Kevin B. 2004. "The Politics of Punishment: Evaluating Political Explanations of Incarceration Rates." *Journal of Politics* 66(3): 925-938.

Sorensen, Jon and Don Stemen. 2002. "The Effect of State Sentencing Policies on Incarceration Rates." *Crime and Delinquency* 48: 456-475.

Spelman, William. 2009. "Crime, Cash, and Limited Options: Explaining the Prison Boom." *Criminology* 8(1): 29-77.

Spohn, Cassia. 2000. "Thirty Years of Sentencing Reform: the Quest for a Racially Neutral Sentencing Process." *Criminal Justice* 3: 427-501.

Spohn, Cassia and David Holleran. 2000. "The Imprisonment Penalty Paid by Young Unemployed Black and Hispanic Male Offenders." *Criminology* 38: 281-306.

Steffensmeier Darrell and Stephen Demuth. 2000. "Ethnicity and Sentencing Outcomes in U.S. Federal Courts: Who Is Punished More Harshly-White, Black, White-Hispanic, or Black-Hispanic Defendants." *American Sociological Review* 65:705–729.

Stemen, Don, Andres Rengifo and James Wilson. 2005. *Of Fragmentation and Ferment: The Impact of State Sentencing Policies on Incarceration Rates, 1975-2002.* Washington, D.C.: U.S. Department of Justice, National Institute of Justice.

Stivers Ireland, Connie. 2001. "Impacts of Discretionary Parole Release on Length of Sentence Served, Percent of Imposed Sentence Served, and Recidivism." Master's thesis. Irvine: University of California.

Stucky, Thomas D. 2005. "Local Politics and Police Strength." *Justice Quarterly* 22:139-169.

Stucky, Thomas D., Karen Heimer and Joseph B. Lang. 2007. "A Bigger Piece of the Pie? State Corrections Spending and the Politics of Social Order." *Journal of Research in Crime and Delinquency* 44(1): 91-123.

Sutton, John R. 2000. "Imprisonment and Social Stratification in Five Common-Law Democracies, 1955-1985." *American Journal of Sociology* 106: 350-386.

Swidler, Ann. 1986. "Culture in Action: Symbols and Strategies." *American Sociological Review* 51(April): 273-286.

Sykes, Gary, Gennaro F. Vito and Karen McElrath. 1987. "Jail Populations and Crime Rates: An Exploratory Analysis." *Journal of Police Science and Administration* 15: 72-77.

Taggart, William A. and Russell G. Winn. 1991. "Determinants of Corrections Expenditures in the American States: An Exploratory Analysis." *Criminal Justice Policy Review* 5(3): 157-182.

Tonry, Michael H. and John C. Coffee. 1987. "Enforcing sentencing guidelines: Plea Bargaining and Review Mechanisms." In *The Sentencing*

Commission and its Guidelines, edited by A. Von Hirsch, K. Knapp and M. Tonry. Boston: Northeastern University Press.

Tonry, Michael H. 2004. *Thinking About Crime: Sense and Sensibility in American Penal Culture*. New York: Oxford University Press.

------. 1997. *Intermediate Sanctions in Sentencing Guidelines*. Washington, D.C.: U.S. Dept. of Justice, National Institute of Justice.

------. 1995. *Malign Neglect: Race, Crime, and Punishment in America*. New York: Oxford University Press.

Travis, Jeremy and Sarah Lawrence. November 2002. *Beyond the Prison Gates: The State of Parole in America*. Washington, D.C.: Urban Institute.

Travis, J. 2007. "Back-end sentencing: A practice in search of a rationale." *Social Research* 74(2): 631-644.

Travis, Jeremy. 2005. *But They All Come Back: Facing the Challenges of Prisoner Reentry*. Washington, D.C.: Urban Institute Press.

Tyler, Tom R. and Robert J. Boeckmann. 1997. "Three Strikes and You Are Out, But Why? The Psychology of Public Support for Punishing Rule Breakers." *Law and Society Review* 31: 237-265.

Ulmer, Jeffery T. and Brian Johnson. 2004. "Sentencing in Context: A Multilevel Analysis." *Criminology* 42(1): 137-177.

Ulmer, Jeffery T. and John H. Kramer. 1998. "The Use and Transformation of Formal Decision-Making Criteria: Sentencing Guidelines, Organizational Contexts, and Case Processing Strategies." *Social Problems* 45(2): 248.

------. 1996. "Court Communities Under Sentencing Guidelines: Dilemmas of Formal Rationality and Sentencing Disparity." *Criminology* 34(3): 383.

United States Department of Justice. Office of Justice Programs. Bureau of Justice Statistics. National Prisoner Statistics, 1978-2011. ICPSR34540-v1. Ann Arbor, MI: Inter-university Consortium for Political and Social Research [distributor], 2013-06-25. http://doi.org/10.3886/ICPSR34540.v1

US Department of Justice. 1973. *Report of the National Advisory Commission on Criminal Justice Standards and Goals*. US Department of Justice: Washington, D.C.

Van Dijk, Jan and Carl H. Steinmetz. 1988. "Pragmatism, Ideology, and Crime Control." Pp. 74-96 in *Public Attitudes to Sentencing*, edited by N. Walker and M. Hough.Grover. Brookfield, VT: Avebury Publishing Co.

Vaughn, Michael S. 1993. "Listening to the Experts: A National Study of Correctional Administrators' Responses to Prison Overcrowding." *Criminal Justice Review* 18: 12-25.

Wacquant, Loic 2009. *Punishing the Poor: The Neoliberal Government of Social Insecurity*. Duke University Press: Durham, NC.

------. 2005. "The Great Penal Leap Backward: Incarceration in America from Nixon to Clinton." Pp. 3-26 in *The New Punitiveness: Current Trends, Theories, Perspectives*, edited by J. Pratt. London: Willan.

------. 2004. *Prisons of Poverty*. Minneapolis, MN: University of Minnesota Press.

------. 2000. "The New 'Peculiar Institution': On the Prison as Surrogate Ghetto." *Theoretical Criminology* 4(3): 377-389.

Weir, Margaret, Ann Shola Orloff, and Theda Skocpol (eds). 1988. *The Politics of Social Policy in the United States*. Princeton, NJ: Princeton University Press.

West, Angela D. and Richard Seiter. 2004. "Social Worker or Cop? Measuring the Supervision Styles of Probation and Parole Officers in Kentucky and Missouri." *Journal of Criminal Justice* 27(2): 27-57.

Western, Bruce. 2006. *Punishment and Inequality in America*. New York: Russell Sage.

Whitman, James Q. 2003. *Harsh Justice: Criminal Policy and the Widening Divide Between America and Europe*. New York: Oxford University Press.

Whitmer, Helen L. 1927. "The History, Theory, and Results of Parole." *Journal of the American Institute of Criminal Law and Criminology*, 18:1 (May): 24-64.

Wilheim, Daniel and Nicholas Turner. 2002. *Issues in Brief: Is the Budget Crisis changing the Way We Look at Sentencing and Incarceration?* New York: Vera Institute of Justice.

Wirth, Louis. 1938. "Urbanism As a Way of Life." *American Journal of Sociology* 44(1): 1-24.

Wooldredge, John and Timothy Griffin. 2005. "Displaced Discretion Under Ohio Sentencing Guidelines." *Journal of Criminal Justice* 33(4): 301-316.

Wooldridge, Jeffrey M. *Econometrics Analysis of Cross Section and Panel Data*. Cambridge, MA: MIT Press.

Wright, Gerald. C., Robert S. Erikson and John P. McIver. 1985. "Measuring State Partisanship and Ideology with Survey Data." *Journal of Politics* 70:469-489.

Xekalaki, Evdokia. 1983. "Hazard Functions and Life Distributions in Discrete Time." *Communications in Statistics*, Part A, (Theory and Methods), 12 (21): 2503-2509.

Yates, Jeff. 1997. "Racial Incarceration Disparity Among States." *Social Science Quarterly* 78: 1001-1010.

Yates, Jeff and Richard Fording. 2005. "Politics and State Punitiveness in Black and White." *Journal of Politics* 67(4): 1099-1121.

Young, Jock. 1999. *The Exclusive Society.* London: Sage.

Zimring, Franklin E. 2001. "Imprisonment Rates and the New Politics of Criminal Punishment." *Punishment and Society* 3: 161-166.

Zimring, Franklin E. and Gordon Hawkins. 1991. *The Scale of Imprisonment.* Chicago: University of Chicago Press.

Index

CPSIA information can be obtained at www.ICGtesting.com
Printed in the USA
BVOW08*0406040915

415284BV00001B/1/P